walking with purpose

Dear Friend,

Who do you see as you look around your neighborhood and community? Look for those who are longing, whether they know it or not, to know the God of the universe. They have not yet learned His character or understood His glory and His love, but they might be willing to receive His inheritance if you were to offer it to them.

This is exactly what Saint Paul did. Jesus had literally knocked him off his feet and changed his life. It was this overwhelming desire to bring this good news to the nations that drove him to cry out in Romans 10:14–15: "But how are men to call upon him in whom they have not believed? And how are they to believe in him of whom they have never heard? And how are they to hear without a preacher? And how can men preach unless they are sent?"

It is the heart behind these verses that inspired the creation of *Passionate Discipleship: A Study of Second Timothy*. After Saint Paul met Jesus on the road to Damascus, he dedicated his entire life to knowing Christ and making Him known to all people and generations. Throughout his travels, Paul invested in several men whom he trained to live as he lived and teach as he taught. Of these men, Timothy was his most beloved friend and disciple.

When we meet Paul in Second Timothy, Paul is sitting in jail for the third time. He knows that he's not getting out alive. He was close to finishing his time on earth and was ready to pass on his ministry. With this in mind, Paul wrote to Timothy with urgency. His goal? To equip Timothy to carry the torch of faith to the next generation and then teach these Christians how to teach others.

Dear sister, this is our call as well. Living for God is a grand adventure! He is the love for which each of us long; once we have found Him, we should not keep His goodness to ourselves. God calls us to be His disciples, say yes to Him without ceasing, and make Him the center of our lives. He also calls us to go forth and bring that message to the world. We are called to be disciples and to make disciples.

We pray that as you immerse yourself in *Passionate Discipleship*, you would receive Paul's invitation to Timothy as your own. Wherever you are in your faith, we invite you to take the next step. Go deeper with the God who loves you and allow Him to equip you to share that love in a way that is true to your gifts and personality.

Lessons 1, 5 and 9 are talks given by Lisa, where she'll share the vision of encountering Christ and then passing the baton of faith on to the next generation. Lessons 2, 3, 4, 6, 7, and 8 are written by Mallory, and will equip you to be discipled by Jesus, and then disciple others. Shorter talks by Mallory will accompany each of those Bible study lessons.

We're so excited to bring this joint project to you! Know that you are in our prayers.

In His Heart,
Lisa Brenninkmeyer and Mallory Smyth

Passionate Discipleship

A Study of 2 Timothy

Lisa Brenninkmeyer and Mallory Smyth

A STUDY OF 2 TIMOTHY

PASSIONATE
Discipleship

Lisa Brenninkmeyer and Mallory Smyth

walking with purpose

SO MUCH MORE THAN A BIBLE STUDY

www.walkingwithpurpose.com

Authored by Lisa Brenninkmeyer and Mallory Smyth

IMPRIMATUR printed paperback + Frank J. Caggiano, Bishop of Bridgeport August 2023

The recommended Bible translations for use in Walking with Purpose™ studies are: The New American Bible, which is the translation used in the United States for the readings at Mass; The Revised Standard Version, Catholic Edition; and The Jerusalem Bible.

Any internet addresses (websites, blogs, etc.) in this book are offered as a resource and may change in the future. Please refer to www.walkingwithpurpose.com as the central location for corresponding materials and references.

23 24 25 26 / 12 11 10 9 8 7 6 5 4 3 2 1

ISBN: 978-1-943173-39-6

Passionate Discipleship: A Study of 2 Timothy

Printed in the United States of America

TABLE OF CONTENTS

Welcome to Walking with Purpose

You have many choices when it comes to how you spend your time—thank you for choosing Walking with Purpose. Studying God's Word with an open and receptive heart will bring spiritual growth and enrichment to all aspects of your life. Every moment you invest will be well worth it.

Each of us comes to this material with a unique vantage point. You are welcome as you are. No previous experience is necessary. Some of you will encounter questions that introduce you to concepts that are new. For others, much of the content will be a review. God meets each one of us where we are. He is always faithful, taking us to a deeper, better spiritual place, no matter where we begin.

The Structure of *Passionate Discipleship*

Passionate Discipleship is a nine-session Bible study that integrates Scripture with the teachings of the Roman Catholic Church to understanding who Jesus is and what that means for us. We will learn how to abide in the wisdom of Christ to navigate the ever-increasing demands and messages of our culture. We will learn what it means to live in the freedom of Christ and how to continually set our minds on Him. This Bible study is designed for both interactive personal study and group discussion.

For those who are participating in Walking with Purpose in a group context, six weeks of this study will be spent in small groups discussing one of the lessons from the *Passionate Discipleship* Bible study guide. During three additional weeks participants will gather for a Connect Coffee, which consists of social time, a video presentation of the related Bible study talk, and small group discussion. Anyone doing this study on her own will find it simplest to watch the videos online, using the URLs provided with the talk outlines. There are also six shorter videos to accompany Lessons 2-4 and 6-8. In a group setting, you may choose to watch these together. If time doesn't allow, we encourage everyone to watch these videos at home as they provide excellent supplemental material.

Study Guide Format and Reference Materials

The *Passionate Discipleship* Bible study guide is divided into three sections:

The first section comprises nine lessons. Most lessons are divided into five "days" to help you form a habit of reading and reflecting on God's Word. If you are a woman who has only bits and pieces of time throughout your day to accomplish tasks, you will find this breakdown of the lessons especially helpful. Each lesson includes an introduction, a conclusion, a resolution section in which you set a goal for yourself based on a theme of the lesson, and portions of the *Catechism of the Catholic Church* (*CCC*) that are referenced in the lesson.

For the three Connect Coffee talks in the series, accompanying outlines are offered as guides for taking notes. Questions are included to guide your group's discussion following the video. The second section, the appendices, contains supplemental materials referred to during the study, as well as an article about Saint Thérèse of Lisieux, the patron saint of Walking with Purpose.

The third section contains the answer key. You will benefit so much more from the Bible study if you work through the questions on your own, searching your heart. This is your very personal journey of faith. The answer key is meant to supplement discussion or provide some guidance when needed.

At the end of the book are pages intended for weekly prayer intentions.

Bible Recommendations

What were your thoughts the first time you picked up a Bible? Perhaps you got one as a gift for Confirmation or graduation. Maybe it was a copy you found lying around at home. It could be that the first time you held a Bible was in a classroom setting. Which of these two statements better reflects how you felt in that moment: *"I just can't wait to dive into these pages because I know it'll be life-changing"* or *"This looks boring and inaccessible. I'm sticking it on my shelf"*? For most of us, it was the latter.

One of our goals at Walking with Purpose is to teach women how to use the Bible as a practical, accessible tool. There are some obstacles to that happening. One problem is how we approach the Bible. If we open it up to Genesis and start reading through from start to finish, we will likely have trouble understanding what is going on (and we'll probably quit once we get into Leviticus). One of the reasons this method can be confusing is because Scripture is not a book; it's a library. This library is filled with many genres: poetry, letters, historical narrative, and apocalyptic writings. When we don't know what genre we are reading, we can quickly become frustrated. For example, reading Genesis as a science book instead of as inspired poetry will cause us to see faith and science at odds. Far too many people write off Christianity because they feel it can't possibly be true after seeing discrepancies between things proven by science and the way those same things are described in the Bible. This is a consequence of not recognizing the Bible as a *library* of Truth, utilizing many genres of literature to lead us to the heart of God, understand His story, and see our place in the epic tale of redemption. Catholics don't read everything in the Bible literally. We read some things literally, but not everything.

Another obstacle to using the Bible as a practical, accessible tool for spiritual growth is not knowing where to begin. This is exactly why Walking with Purpose has created Bible studies and programs like BLAZE. Being guided through Scripture, being led to the passages that are most applicable to life in the twenty-first century, helps the Bible to come alive.

You may also want to consider Bible tabs as a resource. It takes about thirty minutes to put tabs into a Bible, but it makes it so much easier to find your way around Scripture. You can find Bible tabs at Catholic bookstores or online. Be sure to get the Catholic version, as Protestant versions of the Bible are missing seven books. (At the time of the Reformation, the books of Sirach, Tobit, Wisdom, Judith, 1 and 2 Maccabees, and Baruch, as well as portions of Daniel and Esther, were removed in order to embrace a canon of Scripture that reflected Protestant theological beliefs. Books were never added to the Catholic Bible—they have always been there.)

We recommend using either the NABRE (New American Bible Revised Edition) or the RSVCE (Revised Standard Version, Catholic Edition) translations.

Walking with Purpose™ Website

Please visit our website at www.walkingwithpurpose.com to find additional free content, supplemental materials that complement our Bible studies, as well as a link to our online store for additional Bible studies, DVDs, books, and more!

WWP Scripture Printables of our exclusively designed verse cards that compliment all Bible studies. They are available in various sizes and formats, perfect for lock screens or emailing to a friend.

WWP Playlists of Founder Lisa Brenninkmeyer's favorite music accompany each Bible study.

WWP Videos of all Connect Coffee talks.

WWP Blog for a weekly dose of inspiration and encouragement from our bloggers. Subscribe for updates.

WWP Leadership Development Program

Do you long to see more women touched by the love of Christ, but you aren't sure how you can help? We are here to help you learn the art of creating community. It's easier than you think! God doesn't call the equipped; He equips the called. If you love God and love women, then you have what it takes to make a difference in the lives of people around you. Through our training, you'll be empowered to step out of your comfort zone and experience the rush of serving God with passion and purpose. You are not alone, and you can become a great leader. We offer the encouragement and the tools you need to reach out to a world that desperately needs to experience the love of God.

Join Us on Social Media

facebook.com/walkingwithpurpose

twitter.com/walkingwpurpose

instagram.com/walkingwithpurpose_official

youtube.com/walkingwithpurpose_official

pinterest.com/walkingwpurpose

Lessons

 NOTES

Lesson 1: Connect Coffee Talk

THE NEXT GENERATION IS OURS TO RAISE

You can view this talk via the accompanying DVD or digital download purchase, or access it online at walkingwithpurpose.com/videos.

"Paul, an apostle of Christ Jesus by the will of God according to the promise of the life which is in Christ Jesus, to Timothy, my beloved child: Grace, mercy, and peace from God the Father and Christ Jesus our Lord. I thank God whom I serve with a clear conscience, as did my fathers, when I remember you constantly in my prayers. As I remember your tears, I long night and day to see you, that I may be filled with joy. I am reminded of your sincere faith, a faith that dwelt first in your grandmother Lois and your mother Eunice and now, I am sure, dwells in you. For this reason I remind you to rekindle the gift of God that is within you through the laying on of my hands; for God did not give us a spirit of timidity but a spirit of power and love and self-control" (2 Timothy 1:1–7).

Contrasting Two World Views:

Postmodern worldview:

- That truth is relative, that as long as they aren't hurting anyone it doesn't matter what they believe.

- That authority should be respected not just because of a title but only if it's earned.

- That there is no great narrative—no overarching story that makes sense of mankind's struggle.

- That God is irrelevant (if He exists) and that He has nothing relevant to say about our lives.

- "I know" has been replaced by "I feel."

- There is no such thing as human nature (human behavior and psychology are socially determined or constructed).

Christian worldview:

- God exists, loves us, and can be known. He is the supreme reality and exists eternally.

- Absolute truth exists and is essential for the soul.

- When freedom is uncoupled from truth, tyranny results.

- Emphasis on community—we need one another.

- Says there *is* a great narrative—there is an overarching story that makes sense of our struggle.

- Christianity offers an explanation of how things are, how they came to be, and how the world's story will be completed.

The Perennial Questions

- Who am I?

- Why am I here?

- How can I find real love?

- What does it mean to be happy and live a good life?

- How do I focus on what matters and live up to my potential?

- How can I experience lasting peace?

Questions for Discussion

1. As you begin *Passionate Discipleship*, in what way do you want to be made new? How do you want to be changed?

   -feel filled in a way that allows me to pour out to others

2. As you reflect on your own faith journey, was there a person in your life who invited you to ask questions, listened to you, and accompanied you as you wrestled with the answers? If so, what impact did that have on you?

   -my dad in life, arts - but not in faith - Sarah D., Chesy S. but she quit - orchard moms

3. Is there a person in your life whom you are desperate to see set free? Whom you want to know Christ in a real and personal way? What concrete action could you take to be more spiritually intentional in your relationship with that person?

   - Invite B. again to Thomas mom

   - need to reach out to Mere

   - Steph S.

FOR GOD DID NOT GIVE US A SPIRIT OF TIMIDITY BUT a spirit of POWER AND Love AND SELF-CONTROL.

2 TIMOTHY 1:7

Lesson 2

CONFIDENT RELIANCE

Introduction

I recently spent a day in Yorktown, Virginia, the site of the last battle in the American Revolution. I love history and so tried to soak up every moment in this place of great significance. As I walked through a graveyard, I slowed my pace to honor the stories of those who had gone before me. I eventually came across a gravestone that had three full paragraphs of writing. Reading every word, I was blown away by what I learned about this soldier. Before me lay a man who had lived an excellent life. He was joyful and honest, a faithful Christian, and a wonderful family member. This man shone brightly during his life, and it was clear that his loved ones wanted that light to affect anyone who walked past his grave. I left Yorktown inspired to leave a legacy like his, one that would ultimately bring glory to God.

Do you often think about the legacy you want to leave behind? Death seems so far off, so it can be easy for us to forget about it altogether. Without realizing it, we live for the present moment, rarely thinking of eternal things. We fail to consider that how we live will eventually become our legacy. Yet the Catholic Church soberly reminds us, "memento mori"—that is, "remember your death." Psalm 90:12 says, "Teach us to number our days, that we may gain a heart of wisdom." When we know that our days are numbered, we are less likely to live only for survival or pleasure but with attention to what lasts. We are more likely to seek to please God while we are on earth because we know we will meet Him in the next. The more we seek to please Him, the more we will know Him, love Him, and offer His vision for life to those who are coming up behind us. We will grow in spiritual maturity and have wisdom to offer to others.

Saint Paul was reflecting on these same themes as he sat in jail for the third time. He had traveled the known world, fearlessly proclaiming the Gospel. Each time he was arrested, he escaped, living another day to spread the good news of Jesus Christ. This time, however, Paul intuited that he would not again be a free man on this side of eternity.

Throughout Paul's ministry, he poured his life into a few men, whom he also trained to carry the torch of faith beyond his reach. He traveled with them, ate with them, preached with them, and escaped certain death with them. He taught them about Christ, how to pray, how to live as a Christian, and then how to teach the faith to others. Now, with the end so near, Paul's heart and thoughts turned to one of these men, Timothy. He put nib to parchment and wrote his second letter to him.

Paul had met Timothy on his first missionary journey to the small town of Lystra. When he visited Lystra for a second time, he invited Timothy to join him on a mission. During their time together, Timothy became Paul's most trusted companion. In Philippians 2:20–22, Paul showed the high esteem in which he held Timothy: "I have no one else like him, who will show genuine concern for your welfare. For everyone looks out for their own interests, not those of Jesus Christ. But you know that Timothy has proved himself, because as a son with his father he has served with me in the work of the gospel." Paul trusted Timothy so much that he sent him on two missionary journeys, to Thessalonica and Corinth. When Paul wrote this second letter, he had ordained Timothy a bishop to lead the growing church in Ephesus.

Paul knew that Timothy faced incredible obstacles in his role as a bishop. He had to shepherd his flock to stay true to the Gospel of Jesus Christ while contending with the brutality of the Roman empire, guarding them against the false messages threatening to lead them away from Christ and the sin they battled in their own hearts.

Paul, certain of his coming death, was concerned with both the personal and the corporate aspects of the church. Moved with love for Timothy, he wrote a deeply personal and instructive letter. He wanted Timothy to know of his affection. He revealed to Timothy the pain and loneliness he experienced in jail. But most importantly, Paul shared with Timothy everything he wanted Timothy to know in order to live in a faithful relationship with Christ and share the gospel effectively.

Let us remember as we begin reading this book that these are the words of a great man, a fierce saint, facing his last days. Just as we would lean in to hear the last words of our loved ones, let us lean in close and receive all that we can from Paul's letter. Every word, every thought counts.

Day One
A QUICK OVERVIEW OF 2 TIMOTHY

Read 2 Timothy 1:1–7.

Before we begin to move through 2 Timothy, verse by verse, it'll be helpful to get an overview of what Paul is trying to communicate. Let's do this by looking up some key verses throughout the book.

1. Based on 2 Timothy 1:1–4, how would you describe the relationship between Paul and Timothy? Which specific phrases in the passage lead you to that conclusion? *They're close, younger - "persuada" - paternalism*

2. A. What impact did women have on Timothy's spiritual life? See 2 Timothy 1:5.
   grandmother + mother - gives courage as a mom that maybe my kids won't be priests - but legacies are multi-generational

   B. A grandmother and a mother imitated Christ to such a degree that they were able to pass their faith on to the next generation. They didn't shrink back or assume it was someone else's job. In what way would the Holy Spirit have helped them in this regard? See 2 Timothy 1:7. *couro grandmoth wouldn'thae been a peer to Christ - women don't have as much power, so courage/bravery - grace - setting people aflame/conviction despite realities around them walk past fallacy - doesnot make shame*

3. A. Paul recognized that his own flame was going to be extinguished soon. He needed to pass the torch to Timothy, and he needed Timothy to then pass the torch to the next person. With this in mind, what did Paul beg of Timothy in 2 Timothy 1:13? *don't be ashamed*
   - join in suffering for Christ - - Grace, been called to suffer - keep as the pattern of sound teach w/ faith + love

B. Those same instructions are being given to us. We've been entrusted with so many truths in scripture and we're called to follow their pattern—to do it with strength, courage, and consistency. And is this just to benefit ourselves? See 2 Timothy 2:1.

We get taught. We teach others. We teach others to teach others. We keep this pattern of discipleship going. So we're doing two things at the same time: We're being called to follow Christ more closely—to imitate Him faithfully. And at the same time, we're to be talking about Him to others.

4. Doing these two things—being discipled and discipling others—is not done in a vacuum. How are the days we are living in described in 2 Timothy 3:1–7?

We're in the time described in 2 Timothy 4:3–4 when "people will not endure sound teaching, but having itching ears they will accumulate for themselves teachers to suit their own likings and will turn away from listening to the truth and wander into myths." The journey of passionate discipleship won't be easy. There will be obstacles along the way. But as we move through 2 Timothy, I pray that we'll increasingly see that the sacrifice is worth it.

Quiet your heart and enjoy His presence…Soak in His grace, mercy, and peace.

Dear Lord,

I pray that I might have the sincere faith that was seen in Lois and Eunice. I long to be so captivated by love for You, and so transformed by You, that others want to experience what they see in me. But I live in those times of stress described in 2 Timothy 3:1–7. All too often, I love pleasure more than I love You; I listen to all sorts of voices, and I experience confusion as a result. I lack gratitude. The problems aren't just "out there in the culture." I see those things in my own heart.

But I know that You've not placed a spirit of timidity in me—rather, one "of power and love and self-control" (2 Timothy 1:7). So Holy Spirit, please fill me. Transform my selfishness into a willingness to sacrifice for others. Strengthen me to make the choices that while uncomfortable, will usher in needed change. Help me to be grateful for all You have given me. Amen.

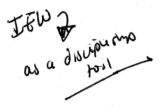

Day Two
THE PROMISE OF LIFE

Reread 2 Timothy 1:1–7.

1. A. How did Paul describe himself at the start of the letter? See 2 Timothy 1:1.

    B. When Paul spoke in verse 1 of the "promise of life that can be found in Christ Jesus," he was talking about something specific. How do John 10:10 and 1 John 5:13 explain this "promise of life"?

2. To understand the significance of Paul's greeting, we need to know a bit about his background. Before his conversion, Paul was Saul of Tarsus. He was a zealous persecutor of the Christian church who experienced a major conversion when he met Jesus on the road to Damascus.

    A. Read Philippians 3:5–6. How did Saint Paul describe the life he had before he gave it to Christ?

    B. In addition to all that Paul listed, he was also wealthy, a dual citizen (Roman and Jewish), and educated under the top rabbi of his time, Galmiel.[1] How did his view of all this prestige change after he met Christ, according to Philippians 3:7–8?

The promise of life Christ offers us is far superior to any other kind of life. In the very first paragraph of the *Catechism of the Catholic Church*, we learn that "God, infinitely perfect, and blessed in Himself, freely created man to share in His own blessed life."[2]

---

[1] "Who is Paul? His Early Life and Why it Matters," Zondervan Blog, Zondervan (12 October, 2016): https:// zondervanacademic.com/blog/who-was-paul-his-early-life-and-why-it-matters.

[2] *CCC* 1.

Take a moment and soak this in. The entire reason that God created you was so that you could live your life in communion with Him, enjoying all that He has to offer. And what does He offer? He offers perfect love and undying faithfulness. He offers joy, peace, and purpose that transcends understanding. Only in Christ will we find our deepest longings satisfied. He offers us a place of refuge from the false identities and trappings of the world. No amount of wealth, beauty, or status can give us complete fullness of life. Only Him.

3. As you reflect on your own life, are you longing for something to be different, but you aren't sure how to bring about needed change? In which area of your life are you yearning for transformation, breakthrough, or healing?

Quiet your heart and enjoy His presence…In Christ, you are a new creation (2 Corinthians 5:17).

Dear Lord,

It's incredible to think about the transformation that Saint Paul experienced. To have gone from zealously persecuting Christians to telling others about Christ is an unbelievable before-and-after story. One of the things that amazes me is that he was able to move past his mistakes. He could have encountered You personally on the road to Damascus and then spent the rest of his life feeling guilty for having gotten things so wrong at the start. But instead, he stayed humbled and got right down to the business of serving You.

Help me to have the same courage. Help me to accept the forgiveness that You so freely offer—the fresh start that is promised in 2 Corinthians 5:17. In You, I am a new creation. The old me is gone. The new me is here. The difference comes from having encountered You. May I see myself through Your eyes. Amen.

Day Three
SINCERE FAITH

Reread 2 Timothy 1:1–7.

(For Days 3–5, we will reread this entire passage and then dive deeper into a few verses.)

1. A. How did Paul describe his worship or service for God, and from whom did he learn that kind of worship? What kind of faith did Timothy have? From where did he get that kind of faith? See 2 Timothy 1:3–5.

   B. It's significant that Saint Paul pointed out the long-term impact of the faith of the women in Timothy's family. Can you speculate about what kind of women they must have been?

In the Christian world, many have embraced the concept that faith can be lived out between "me and Jesus." Saint Paul tells us that while faith is personal, it is not simply private and individual. Recalling the faith he and Timothy received from their ancestors, he reminds us that the Gospel message is transmitted through relationships. It is not experienced in a vacuum. For better or worse, our personalities, beliefs, and actions are profoundly affected by what has been passed down to us through our families.

2. A. What does the *Catechism of the Catholic Church* say about the importance of the parental role in passing on education to children? See *CCC* 2221.

   B. Describe how the *Catechism of the Catholic Church* directs parents to pass the legacy of their faith to their children. See *CCC* 2226.

3. A. For some of us, our families have passed a beautiful faith on to us. When we think of our parents or grandparents, we think of men and women who had a steadfast love for God and lived it well. Who from your family witnessed to the truth of the Gospel and the beauty of faith?

   B. For others, our family experience has been a major barrier to our faith. Our mothers and fathers failed to be examples of divine love. They did not exhibit love for God or did not make it a priority to pass it on to us. What kind of negative witness did your family give you?

Either way, it's important for us to understand the impact that our family's faith has had on us. The more we understand how our family's legacy has shaped our worldview and our faith, the better we can make sense of it. We can learn what to accept and what we need to reject so that we can better grab hold of the promise of life found in Jesus Christ.

CCC 239 sheds light on how God can heal any incorrect understanding of His love that our parents might have given us: "The language of faith thus draws on the human experience of parents, who are in a way the first representatives of God for man. But this experience also tells us that human parents are fallible and can disfigure the face of fatherhood and motherhood. We ought therefore to recall that God transcends the human distinction between the sexes. He is neither man nor woman: he is God. He also transcends human fatherhood and motherhood, although he is their origin and standard: no one is father as God is Father." The biggest part of that for me is the fact that "no one is father as God is Father."

4. What kind of faith did you receive from your family? How has it shaped your worldview? In what ways did your parents or family members give you a positive understanding of faith? In what ways did your family give you a negative or false understanding of Christianity? If so, how?

Quiet your heart and enjoy His presence…You are included in His legacy.

1 John 3:1: "See what love the Father has given us, that we should be called children of God; and so we are."

Dear Lord,

There is no life better than the one You offer to me. At every moment, You draw near to me, beckoning me to live, move, and have my being as a woman who belongs completely to You. Help me to notice You more. Help me to draw nearer to You. I know You called those who came before me to the same destiny, and I thank You for the ways my family has shown me an accurate picture of who You are. Thank You for the ways that they have taught me who You are, what You are like, and how to know You and love You through Your Church. And for the ways that they have failed, Lord, I forgive them in Your name. Please come into my heart, my memories, and my understanding of You. Please fill in the gaps of the legacy I have received from my family so that your love can create a new kind of legacy, one that flows into those around me and brings forth a sincere and lasting faith. You are the perfector of faith. You never leave us without all that we need to live completely and fully in you. Thank you for Your presence in my life, Lord Jesus; awaken me to see You at work around me. Become the legacy that I leave for those hereafter. I love You, Lord; help me to love You more. Amen.

Day Four
REKINDLE THE GIFT

Reread 2 Timothy 1:1–7.

1. What did Paul command Timothy to do with the gift of God within him? How did Timothy receive that gift? See 2 Timothy 1:6.

In Paul's greeting, he testified to Timothy's robust faith—the faith that began as a beautiful inheritance reached a new maturity when Saint Paul and a gathering of elders laid hands on him and ordained him the bishop of Ephesus.[3]

2. A. We have not only received a legacy of faith from our family, but many of us, like Timothy, have received the fullness of God's divine life and the deposit of the Holy Spirit through the sacraments. Read *CCC* 1121. What three sacraments confer a sacramental character, or "seal," and a sharing in Christ priesthood? How do they impact those who receive them?

Timothy received the fullness of grace and the seal of the Holy Spirit through the

---

[3] Scott Hahn, Curtis Mitch, *The Letters of St. Paul to the Thessalonians, Timothy, and Titus* (San Francisco: Ignatius Press, 2010), 45.

sacrament of Holy Orders, priestly ordination. In Holy Orders, men share in the one priesthood of Jesus Christ, his mediating role between God and humanity. Laypeople also receive the seal of the Holy Spirit in the sacrament of Confirmation. Confirmation is a kind of commissioning—making you capable of being sent on an official mission to represent, in a spiritually mature way, Christ.

B. One of the symbols of the Holy Spirit is fire. How is the Holy Spirit compared to fire, according to *CCC* 696?

Years ago I heard a priest speak of the many Catholics who had received the sacrament of Confirmation. He reflected that millions of people are walking around with gifts of the Holy Spirit buried within them. The fire had gone into their hearts, but God's people never fanned its flame. The fire faded and the people did not live transformed.

3. A. Mother Angelica famously said, "If people would truly live out their Catholic faith, the world would change overnight." Think about the number of men and women who have gotten their sacraments and left the church or have stayed but are merely going through the motions. Take a moment and daydream with God about what your parish would look like if it "caught fire." Name three things you wish would "start burning."

B. Take a moment to reflect on your personal experience. Have you received the sacrament of Confirmation? Why or why not? Have you taken responsibility for the gift of God that has been given to you? What is a specific action you can take to "fan into flame" or take "ownership" of the gifts poured into your heart by the Holy Spirit?

Quiet your heart and enjoy His presence...Invite Him to kindle a fire in your soul.

Dear Lord,

Please help me to see where the fire in my heart has dimmed or gone out. I want to have the same passion and desire for You that I had at first. Whatever breaks your heart, I want it to break mine too. Awaken in me an awareness of the suffering people around me. Grant me the grace to make a difference in the places where You are calling me to be Your hands and feet.

There are times that I feel worn out from caring, serving, and interacting with all the needs around me. So I'm coming to you and asking You to pour the oil of Your Holy Spirit onto the kindling of my heart so that the flames are from You. May You be the fuel that propels me forward. Give me Your compassion, Your love, Your patience, Your kindness. I want to be a conduit so the fire of Your love reaches those around me. Amen.

Day Five
THE SPIRIT OF POWER, LOVE, AND SELF-CONTROL

Reread 2 Timothy 1:1–7.

1. In 2 Timothy 1:7, Saint Paul is explaining what the Holy Spirit is like. This Spirit dwells inside every Christian. How would you describe the Spirit based on this verse?

"Do not be afraid" is the most frequent command in the Bible.[4] It's almost as if God knew that, in our brokenness, we were prone to let a spirit of fear rule us. Fear itself is an amoral physical reaction to a danger meant to keep us safe, but the spirit of fear is different.

2. When we give ourselves over to the spirit of fear, we end up living in a constant state of fight or flight and the impact of chronic fear begins to take its toll on our physiology. Fear decreases our ability to regulate emotions and to think before acting. Mentally, the spirit of fear leads people into chronic fatigue and clinical depression.[5] It is not from God. It binds us and holds us back. It limits our freedom and prevents us from experiencing the abundant life God desires for us.

---

[4] "The Most Frequent Command in the Bible," Body Tithe (28 February, 2023): https://bodytithe.com/frequent-command-bible/.

[5] "Impact of Fear and Anxiety," University of Minnesota, Taking Charge of Your Health and Well-being (15 November, 2022): https://www.takingcharge.csh.umn.edu/impact-fear-and-anxiety.

We can find ourselves gripped by the spirit of fear for any number of reasons. Many of us struggle with anxiety or have suffered traumas through no fault of our own. Whatever your story, please know that you are not alone. The Lord does not stand on the outside of our fear and demand we step out of it. He enters into it and walks us step by step toward one more degree of freedom.

Knowing that you are not alone, that fear is a natural response to a broken world, and that the Lord offers you His ever-present hand, is there an area of your life over which the spirit of fear hovers? Reflect on what you are afraid of, why, and how this fear is affecting you.

3. Instead of living in a spirit of fear, Paul invited Timothy to live in the Holy Spirit, who gives us power, love, and self-control. Raise your hand if you'd prefer to be in possession of these qualities! To learn more about how the Holy Spirit helps us to overcome fear, you can read Appendix 3.

After Jesus ascended to Heaven, the apostles became terrified of the Roman government. Hiding all together, they received the Holy Spirit as tongues of fire landed on their heads. Their fear transformed to boldness as they went out and began the movement that would one day bring the Gospel to the ends of the earth (Acts 2:1–13). This is the **power** that we can find in the Holy Spirit.

In Matthew 5:44, Jesus commands us to "Love your enemies and pray for those who persecute you." This kind of **love** that transcends all natural inclinations can only be achieved through the Holy Spirit.

1 Corinthians 10:13 says, "No temptation has overtaken you that is not common to man. God is faithful, and he will not let you be tempted beyond your strength, but with the temptation will also provide the way of escape, that you may be able to endure it." That *way out* is the power of the Holy Spirit, which enables us to practice **self-control**. The word used for self-control is *sophronismos*, which can be translated as the "sanity of saintliness."[6] It is only through the Holy Spirit that we can gain mastery over our passions and direct them toward saintly living.

---

[6] William Barclay, *The Letters to Timothy, Titus, and Philemon* (Louisville, KY: Westminster John Knox Press, 2017), 162.

Do you need more power, deeper love, or more self-control? In what area of your life or in relation to what? Write about it here, and take a moment to ask the Holy Spirit to pour Himself into you and give you the gift of these graces.

Quiet your heart and enjoy His presence…He places His spirit within you.

Dear Lord,

I come to You today with a new awareness of your presence within me. Through the faith that has been passed down to me and through my participation in Your Church, You have given me the gift of Your Holy Spirit. At this moment, I accept Your gift with all my heart, with all my mind, and with all my strength. I ask You to fan the flame, no matter how dim, into a blazing fire. I give You permission to burn so brightly in me that those who come into contact with me cannot help but be transformed by You. Please show me how You want me to rekindle that gift on a daily basis and give me the grace of obedience so that I can keep living by my yes to You. I give You permission to rid me of the things in my life that keep me from rekindling this great gift. I lay all my fears before You, especially the fear of [ ]. I declare that they are not of the Holy Spirit and should have no place in my life. Please replace them with Your power, Your love, and Your self-control. In the words of Your Church, "Come, Holy Spirit, fill the hearts of your faithful, and enkindle in us the fire of your love. Send forth your Spirit, and we shall be created, and you shall renew the face of the earth." Amen.

Conclusion

As we think about Paul's relationship with Timothy, I wonder how long it took for him to earn the right to speak in such a way that he could challenge Timothy to do hard things. There must have been countless interactions first that were characterized by encouragement. Why do I believe this to be true? Because we are best coached by someone who we are certain has our best interests at heart.

Could it be that this is one of the reasons Lois and Eunice had such an influence on Timothy? They loved him in a way that only a grandmother and mother can and cared about every aspect of his life. When that unconditional love was combined with two examples of holiness, a compelling witness emerged. Timothy wanted what he could see they had—a vibrant life resulting from following Christ.

As we reflect on our own lives, let's make sure that our relationships are first characterized by unconditional support and encouragement. How can we interact with people in such a way that they feel beloved by us? What heartening words could we speak to the weary? How can we call out the goodness we see in people, even when at the same time we can see how far they need to go? Our words have power. When we pour into relationships and are soft places for hearts to land, we earn the right to speak truth. But the love, grace, mercy, and peace need to be offered first.

In the next lesson, we're going to start moving into some of Paul's instructions. He's going to encourage Timothy not to be ashamed and to be willing to suffer. I can imagine it was a hard transition to go from encouraging to exhorting. The only way we'll be able to make that same transition is if we are relying on the Holy Spirit.

In whatever we face, whether it be a hard personal choice between imitating Christ, doing what feels more comfortable, or speaking truth when it would be easier to stay silent, let's lean into the truth of 2 Timothy 1:7. "God did not give us a spirit of timidity but a spirit of power and love and self-control." What we lack, He will provide. James 4:2 says there are times when "you do not have, because you do not ask." Let's go to God with His unlimited supply of grace, asking Him to release a supernatural power within us that "is able to do far more abundantly than all we ask or think" (Ephesians 3:20).

Want to learn more about this topic? Don't miss this lesson's short video from Mallory at walkingwithpurpose.com/videos.

My Resolution

"My Resolution" is your opportunity to write down one specific, personal application from this lesson. We can take in a lot of information from studying the Bible, but if we don't translate it into action, we have totally missed the point. In James 1:22, we're told that we shouldn't just hear the Word of God; we are to "do what it says." So what qualities should be found in a good resolution? It should be **personal** (use the pronouns I, *me*, *my*, *mine*); it should be **possible** (don't choose something so far-fetched that you'll just become discouraged); it should be **measurable** (a specific goal to achieve within a specific time period); and it should be **action oriented** (not just a spiritual thought).

Examples:

1. I will spend thirty to sixty minutes in Adoration, praying with the Lord about the kind of faith or understanding of Catholicism that I received from my family. I will write down the ways that my family's legacy brought me close to God and where their legacy brought barriers to faith or confusion about God's character. I will bring these notes to prayer and ask God to reveal His true self to me and to heal the wounds that have been passed down in my family.

2. I will take some time to journal about the kind of legacy I want to leave behind for those who will outlive me. I will then honestly assess whether the way that I am living right now will lead to that kind of legacy. I will ask the Lord what I need to change about my life to make that legacy possible.

3. I will examine the ways that I tell myself that I am not worthy of God's forgiveness. I will then choose to believe that Jesus abolished the power of sin and death over my life, in every aspect of my life. I will receive the sacrament of Confession, forgive myself as God has forgiven me, and ask Him for the grace to live in a newfound freedom.

My Resolution:

Catechism Clips

CCC 696 Fire. While water signifies birth and the fruitfulness of life given in the Holy Spirit, fire symbolizes the transforming energy of the Holy Spirit's actions. The prayer of the prophet Elijah, who "arose like fire" and whose "word burned like a torch," brought down fire from Heaven on the sacrifice on Mount Carmel. This event was a "figure" of the fire of the Holy Spirit, who transforms what he touches. John the Baptist, who goes "before [the Lord] in the spirit and power of Elijah," proclaims Christ as the one who "will baptize you with the Holy Spirit and with fire." Jesus will say of the Spirit: "I came to cast fire upon the earth; and would that it were already kindled!" In the form of tongues "as of fire," the Holy Spirit rests on the disciples on the morning of Pentecost and fills them with himself. The spiritual tradition has retained this symbolism of fire as one of the most expressive images of the Holy Spirit's actions. "Do not quench the Spirit."

CCC 1121 The three sacraments of baptism, confirmation, and holy orders confer, in addition to grace, a sacramental character or "seal" by which the Christian shares in Christ's priesthood and is made a member of the church according to different states and functions. This configuration to Christ and to the church, brought about by the Spirit, is indelible. It remains forever in the Christian as a positive disposition for grace, a promise, a guarantee of divine protection, and a vocation to divine worship and to the service of the Church. Therefore, these sacraments can never be repeated.

CCC 2221 The fecundity of conjugal love cannot be reduced solely to the procreation of children, but it must extend to their moral education and their spiritual formation. "The role of parents in education is of such importance that it is almost impossible to provide an adequate substitute." The right and the duty of parents to educate their children are primordial and inalienable.

CCC 2226 Education in the faith by the parents should begin in the child's earliest years. This already happens when family members help one another to grow in faith by the witness of a Christian life in keeping with the Gospel. Family catechesis precedes, accompanies, and enriches other forms of instruction in the faith. Parents have the mission of teaching their children to pray and to discover their vocation as children of God. The parish is the Eucharistic community and the heart of the liturgical life of Christian families; it is a privileged place for the catechesis of children and parents.

Verse Study

See Appendix 4 for instructions on how to complete a verse study.

Ephesians 1:18

1. Verse: _I pray your heart will be flooded with light so you can understand the confident hope he has given to them he called — his holy people who are (his glorious inheritance —)_

2. Paraphrase:

3. Questions: _If we are his inheritance — or gods — than the works of disciple but — is the greatest behavior_

4. Cross-references:

5. Personal Application:

NOTES

Lesson 3

CALLED TO MAKE DISCIPLES

Introduction

Can you think of someone whose personal investment in others has created a ripple effect far beyond that person's "expected" reach? What did they do, and what was the impact? Emily

I met such a woman when I was fourteen years old. A young mother in her early thirties, she was joyful, kind, and brilliant. Her love for Jesus was magnetic, and until then, I'd never met anyone like her.

Over the next ten years, some friends and I would spend hours sitting with her at her kitchen table. We ate her food and babysat her children while she poured her life into ours, generously listening to our teenage angst and teaching us how to follow Jesus.

Twenty years later, it is staggering. No, not every person who sat at her table stayed Catholic. But those who did are bringing the gospel all over the word—far beyond the reach of her kitchen. One of these friends became a missionary and then a religious sister. Another attended the Divine Mercy University and is bringing the gospel into her psychology practice. And I, after a brief detour from my faith, have been in full lay apostolate work for over ten years.

This woman continued to share her faith long after I graduated high school. Not only did she continue to share her life and her love of Christ with young students, she brought that love into her friendships with adult women as she invited them into her home for Bible study. Many people from my hometown owe her a direct debt of gratitude for their love for Jesus and their ability to share Him with others.

Although she never formally defined what she was doing, she made disciples and taught them to make disciples. She didn't do it from a stage; she didn't have a social media platform or a PhD in theology. And with four young daughters, she didn't even have time. She had a deep faith, a welcoming home, and a community. She developed authentic friendships and then shared her greatest love, Jesus, with her friends. And all the while she taught them to follow her example. It's incredible what God will do with someone who shares their faith with others and teaches them how to do the same.

When people teach others how to follow Christ and then teach them how to teach others, they participate in spiritual multiplication. The Fellowship of Catholic University Students (FOCUS) likes to illustrate the effectiveness of spiritual multiplication with the example of the super evangelist and the everyday person who disciples just two people, teaching them to disciple two people.

If the super evangelist makes one million disciples per year, at the end of the thirty-third year, the super evangelist will have brought thirty-three million people to Christ.

If the everyday person invests in two people, then those two people invest in two more people and that pattern continues for thirty-three years, that discipleship chain will have reached every person on the face of the earth in thirty-three years.[7] Incredible.

As we begin the second chapter of second Timothy, let us remember what is going on. Paul is near the end of his life, writing to Timothy from jail. He was imparting everything he thought Timothy needed to hear to carry the torch of faith. As bishop of Ephesus, Timothy had to guide his young church through many obstacles. As we will see, many false teachers taught false messages, which confused the faithful. Paul gave Timothy instructions on how to combat them.

At the beginning of this chapter, Paul gave Timothy one of his most important instructions. He told him in 2 Timothy 2:2: "And what you have heard from me before many witnesses entrust to faithful men who will be able to teach others also." This is exactly what Paul had done with Timothy. Paul invested deeply in Timothy's life. They had forged a true friendship with Christ at the center. Even more, Paul entrusted

---

[7] Dr. Brian McAdam, "Making Disciples of All Nations Through Spiritual Multiplication" FOCUS (30 April, 2012): https://focusequip.org/making-disciples-of-all-nations-through-spiritual-multiplication/.

Timothy with all he had learned and also taught Timothy how to bring that message to others. Paul was instructing Timothy to be a spiritual multiplier, the best and most effective way to spread the gospel message through all cultures and generations.

While evangelizing is daunting to many Catholics, we do not have to be, nor are many of us called to be, the "super evangelists" from the example above. Isn't that a relief? We do not need to overcomplicate evangelization. All of us are called to be disciples, make disciples, and teach others how to make disciples. How do we do this? We start from where we are: we invest deeply in our communities, in our neighborhoods, at local events, and from our kitchen tables. It's simple, each of us is called to it, and it begins with faithfulness to Christ.

Day One
THE CALL TO EMBODY THE GOSPEL

Read 2 Timothy 1:8–11.

1. A. What three instructions did Paul give Timothy in 2 Timothy 1:8?

    ① Don't be ashamed
    ② join w/ me in suffering   ③ rely on power of God

    B. Paul encouraged Timothy to take his share of suffering for the gospel in the power of God. How should that impact our expectations around comfort and suffering in our own lives? Have you ever experienced the power of God in the midst of your suffering? If so, describe it here. *my thot: I want everything to be comfortable then Evangelize*

2. What three things did God do for us according to 2 Timothy 1:9?

    Working mom's zoom 8:30 - 9:30

3. A. How did God reveal His grace and accomplish His saving work according to 2 Timothy 1:10? *Christ Jesus, abolishing death - and brought Immortality to light*

The Hebrew word Paul used to describe how Jesus abolished death is *katargeo*, which means to deprive of force, influence, and power.[8] Jesus deprived your sin, no matter how bad—no matter how dark, no matter how disqualifying you think it is—of its eternal consequences. Because of what He did, you are no longer defined by your sin's power. You are not beholden to sin's tyranny. Christ's power dissipates the power of sin. By Christ's saving work, you are restored to the Father.

> B. What does it mean in your life right now that Jesus abolished death? Do you believe it? Why or why not? *I can trust him – The obstacles of this world are secondary to him – He is eternal*

> C. Have you truly accepted God's grace in your life? Are you condemning yourself more than God is condemning you? Ask Him to take away that guilt and shame that you carry and replace it with the grace of restoration.
> *I suppose – my to do lists keep me from him / a cry of guilt. I can't see another way besides anger.*

4. A. The verses we just read awaken us to God's grace, which comes with a holy calling. How does the Catholic Church define grace? What is our calling? See *CCC* 1996.

While each of us is created for a unique purpose, there is a common calling we all share—the call to holiness. William Barclay explains, "Those who have known the saving power of the gospel are changed men and women, in their work, their leisure, their home life, and in their character. There should be an essential difference between Christians and non-Christians, because Christians have obeyed the summons to walk the road to holiness."[9]

> B. The call to holiness is universal for all of us, but each of us is called to live out the gospel according to our unique gifts. How did Saint Paul live and share the gospel according to 2 Timothy 1:11?
> *Herald, Apostle, Teacher*

---

[8] "Bible Study Tools: Katargeo" (16 November, 2022): https://www.biblestudytools.com/lexicons/greek/nas/katargeo.html.

[9] Barclay, 165.

5. Pastor John Mark Comer described obedience to God as doing what Jesus would do if He were you. What is your life like right now? How is God asking you to live transformed in your work, leisure, home life, and character? What would Jesus do if He were you? *The work in front of me — not worrying about tmw*

Quiet your heart and enjoy His presence…He can make you worthy of the call you have received.

Dear Lord,

In the words of Pastor Tim Keller, "I am more sinful and flawed in myself than I ever dared believe, yet at the very same time I am more loved and accepted in Jesus Christ than I ever dared hope."[10] Help me to see that this is the best news in the world. This news means forgiveness. It means freedom and a new, true identity. No longer do I need to pretend to be someone I am not. No longer do I need to try to measure up to everyone else or compete with other women in my community. We all start from the same place, in desperate need of a savior. But You did not just leave us to that need. Through your life, death, and resurrection, You turned everything upside down. You became a man. Death lost its power. You restored me to God's family, the family for which I was made. Lord, how great a savior You are. I offer You all my worship. I lay before You the broken parts of me and fearlessly accept Your unending mercy. By your power, I choose to stake my life on this truth. Lord, I choose to make You and the gospel message the center of my life, the place from which I see the world, and how I conduct my daily affairs. Please keep this truth in front of me so that I can slowly but surely be more conformed to Your reality and Your will. You're so good. Thank you for transforming even the worst sin into an avenue of grace. Amen.

---

[10] Timothy and Kathy Keller, *The Meaning of Marriage: Facing the Complexities of Commitment with the Wisdom of God* (New York City: Penguin Publishing Group, 2013) 44.

Day Two
GUARD THE TRUTH

Read 2 Timothy 1:12–14.

1. A. Read 2 Timothy 1:12. Why had Paul suffered and what enabled him to endure it?

It is not a matter of *if* the Christian life will come at a cost, but *when*. Living for God requires that we reject any belief system or action that goes against the gospel. Consequently, we will eventually have to say or do something unpopular. We will have to give up something we want or allow our reputation to be unfairly tarnished. For some believers who live in countries where Christianity is outright illegal, the stakes are high. For others, the stakes are a bit lower, as Christianity is seen as weird, backward, and bigoted. If we are going to serve God, however, we have to stop our service to everything that goes against Him. This means that we will inevitably suffer. We are called to get comfortable with discomfort.

B. How much would you be willing to endure to stay true to your faith in Christ? Would you be willing to be seen as weird or backward? Would you be willing to speak the truth, even if you might be misunderstood? Would you be willing to be left out of social invitations because you are serious about Christianity? Would you be willing to live with much less than your peers? Explore what the line is for you and why you've put it there.

Working on the Porno – makes space for discipleship – with less is buy now-things

2. A. After Paul proclaimed his unending trust in God, what did he tell Timothy to do in 2 Timothy 1:13–14? *Hold to the standard of truth – sound teaching – with faith ; Guard the good – w/ holy spirit*

Throughout this passage, Saint Paul continually draws us back to the theme of guarding and entrusting. The word that Saint Paul uses for entrust is *paratheke,* which means "a deposit committed to someone's trust."[11]

---

[11] Barclay, 169.

With God, *paratheke* is reciprocal. On one hand, God asks us to entrust ourselves to Him. But on the other hand, God entrusts Himself to us. Consider this depth of meaning. God, who is all powerful and all perfect, entrusts the treasure of faith to His people. He gives us the gift of faith, a vote of confidence, and then trusts us with His message. We can honor and guard the faith or neglect and defile it. Will we be responsive? Will we be responsible with what has been entrusted to us?

This hit home — kids given opportunity that they ignore —

B. What does it mean to you that God has entrusted Himself and His teaching to you? Is there something He has given to you that you need to entrust to *Him* for safekeeping? *my time + plans*

3. A. In our world we are inundated with different teachings and competing messages. What has the Church given to us, and how does it help us "guard the treasure that has been entrusted to us"? Read *CCC* 84. *Eucharist —*

B. Are you guarding your sacred deposit well? If so, how? Name some practices that protect this treasure. If not, in ways are you being careless? What are some things in your life that you might have to get rid of so that you can better guard the truth entrusted to you?

Quiet your heart and enjoy His presence...You belong to Him; He will guard your heart and mind.

Dear Lord,

There are so many teachings that are competing for my attention, and their promises are appealing. The lure of comfort, wealth, and status tug on my heart. Trendy beliefs draw me in and tempt me to downplay the faith that You have given to me. Give me the eyes to see through these things for the empty promises that they are. Give me the grace of endurance and the conviction of heart that make me ready and willing to guard your Truth no matter the cost. Lord, these are big asks, and in many ways, I don't even want to have to guard your Truth to the point of discomfort. But I want to want it! I know that by the power of the Holy Spirit, you can make me more faithful than I am right now and more courageous than I think I can be. Your word tells me that if You begin a good work in me, You will see it through to the end. I am entrusting myself completely to you Lord. I give you the authority to do what You want in my life to make me worthy of the entrustment You have given to me. Amen.

Day Three
NAVIGATING CHRISTIAN COMMUNITY

Read 2 Timothy 1:15–18.

1. As Saint Paul continued to write to Timothy from jail, he began to reveal his personal heartaches. What did he share with Timothy in 2 Timothy 1:15?

   Rejection - places where he had footholds, but they crumbled - trust God's purpose - let go

Saint Paul had loved the people in his community with an abiding love. In 1 Thessalonians 2:8, Saint Paul reveals that love when he says, "So, being affectionately desirous of you, we were ready to share with you not only the gospel of God but also our own selves, because you had become very dear to us."

Saint Paul had shared his deepest self with his friends, but his multiple arrests created too much pressure for them. Scholars believe that when push came to shove, members of the Christian church disassociated from Saint Paul not because of theological disagreement, but because they didn't want to become guilty by association. They were afraid. The more Saint Paul had trouble with the law, the more tarnished his reputation became. So not wanting to land in jail themselves, Saint Paul's friends abandoned him.

2. Saint Paul experienced the same feeling that Jesus experienced before His Passion. Read Mark 14:50. What happened to Jesus when he was arrested and suddenly association with Him became risky?

3. A. Can you relate to how Phygelus and Hermogenes might have felt? What are the risks of staying loyal to your faith or to someone you know who is experiencing problems because of what they believe?

fear - clouds trust - causes us to grasp at control over person

not guy to Holy spirit -

- vine + branch -
· see you as invaluable
· pushing -

B. What do you think is the difference between setting up healthy boundaries in relationships and abandoning them when circumstances become difficult?

Still praying for - accepting rejection.

C. Can you relate to how Saint Paul felt? Describe a time in your life when you felt abandoned. How would things have been different if your family or friends had been loyal to you in that difficult time?

honestly - no - not really

my Dad's death - but not disloyal - a few clicks that get kicked off

4. A. Although many had abandoned Saint Paul, some had stayed close to him. Who does Saint Paul mention in 2 Timothy 1:16–18?

B. Can you think of a time in your life when someone was loyal to you when everyone else seemed to disappear? How did that loyalty affect you?

can't imagine being raised as an abandoner or all scripture/History

Quiet your heart and enjoy His presence…Even when no one else is faithful, He is faithful.

Dear Lord,

You gave everything for us, and in your darkest moments, your friends abandoned you. They were fearful of the harm that association with You might cause. Lord, I relate to them. So often I am tempted to leave when relationships become difficult or situations are hard to manage. I ask you for the gift of fortitude to stay faithful to my loved one as long as You called me to be faithful. Help me to stay faithful to You always. Lord, in Your name, I also forgive the people in my life who have left me when I needed them. Help me to see things from their perspective and offer them the compassion you offer me. You tell me in Isaiah 49:15 that You will never forget me. Help me to recognize that even if I feel alone, I am never alone. I am never abandoned. You always draw near. You are always the one who initiates communion with me. Make me aware of that communion at all times and give me the grace to always respond to You, Lord, with faithfulness. Amen.

Day Four
MISSIONARY DISCIPLES

Read 2 Timothy 2:1–7.

1. What two things did Paul tell Timothy to do in 2 Timothy 2:1–2?

Each time I sit before the Blessed Sacrament when I travel, or hear the Mass said in a different language, I think of Jesus's command to make disciples of all nations in Matthew 28:19. Two thousand years later, we are witnesses to the apostles' faithfulness to commands like 2 Timothy 2:2. Throughout the ages, God's faithful spent their lives teaching the truth to others and training them to pass on that truth so that we could receive the same gospel generations later.

What will we do now that it's our turn? Father Mike Schmitz gives us this description of disciples and disciple makers: "A disciple is someone who changes their schedule to follow Jesus. A disciple maker is someone who changes their schedule to help someone else follow Jesus."[12]

Will we, like Timothy and other giants of the faith, change our schedules to follow Christ and help others to do so?

2. A. It's uncomfortable to share our faith with others, mostly because we don't know where to begin. How do you feel about Paul's exhortation to "entrust the faith to faithful men who will be able to teach others also"? What inspires you to want to share the Gospel? What holds you back?

Pope Francis boldly challenged us to accept this glorious responsibility in his apostolic exhortation, *Evangelii Gaudium*:

Every Christian is challenged, here and now, to be actively engaged in

---

[12] Father Mike Schmitz, "Why Make Disciples," YouTube, Catholic Archdiocese of Sidney (8 June, 2022): https://www.youtube.com/watch?v=SzU5PaE8lDs.

evangelization; indeed, anyone who has truly experienced God's saving love does not need much time or lengthy training to go out and proclaim that love. Every Christian is a missionary to the extent that he or she has encountered the love of God in Christ Jesus: we no longer say that we are "disciples" and "missionaries," but rather that we are always "missionary disciples." If we are not convinced, let us look at those first disciples, who, immediately after encountering the gaze of Jesus, went forth to proclaim him joyfully: "We have found the Messiah!" (John 1:41).[13]

B. Sharing the gospel always begins with sharing our personal encounter with Christ. This is familiar territory! It is your own life. Take a moment and write about the difference that Jesus has made in your life. Then write down three people in your life with whom you could share your story.

3. A. This kind of work is not for the faint of heart. Paul illustrated the intensity of the Christian life using three metaphors. Describe the first one according to 2 Timothy 2:3–4.

Enlisting in the army means a new mode of life. No longer can a soldier focus on civilian life. Civilians take pleasure in food, drink, and comfort, but soldiers maintain a strict diet and a rigorous training schedule. Civilians busy themselves with varying affairs, while soldiers devote themselves primarily to the orders of their commander.

B. Read 2 Timothy 2:5. Describe the second metaphor for the Christian life.

For someone to win a game, they have to know the rules and abide by them. If they

---

[13] Pope Francis, *The Joy of the Gospel* (Rome, Italy. Vatican Press: 2013), paragraph 120.

decide that they don't like the rules and don't follow them, they are not actually playing the game and will be disqualified altogether.

C. Are there parts of God's game plan that you are trying to change to make your life easier?

D. What is the third metaphor that Paul used for the Christian life in 2 Timothy 2:6–7? Why should the hardworking farmer receive the first shares of the crops?

Quiet your heart and enjoy His presence…He has blessed you to be a blessing.

Dear Lord,

In a world that throws a million things at me to compete for my attention, help me focus my attention completely on You. In a world that tells me that I can play by my own rules, give me the grace to find freedom in obedience to You. The world entices me toward comfort over discipline. Remind me that I was not made for comfort but for greatness. Help me to remember that in every aspect of the Christian life, You offer me the blessings of transformation. You promise that the more I focus on You, the more closely I follow You, the more like You I will become. And the more like You I become, the more that others will see You at work in my life. Thank you, Lord, for all the ways that You have blessed me by offering me Your presence. Thank you for all the times that You have transformed me to look more like You even when I couldn't see it. You are forming me into a "little Christ," and the story of that transformation is meant to be shared. Lord, I ask you to lead me into relationships and to open up opportunities to share what You have done in my life. I don't always have the perfect words to say, but You promise in Matthew 10:19 that You will give me the words. I don't always have the courage. Help me to trust and lean into the courage that You will give me. You have blessed me to be a blessing to others. I give You permission to use me however You want to open up Your blessings to the world. Amen.

Day Five
REMEMBER JESUS CHRIST

Read 2 Timothy 2:8–10.

1. Read 2 Timothy 2:8. In what two ways did Paul describe Jesus Christ?

There is great significance in Paul's description of Jesus as both raised from the dead and a descendant of David. Throughout the Old Testament, there are hundreds of prophecies that describe the coming Messiah. Among them are the predictions that the Messiah would be born of the line of King David (2 Samuel 7:12–13), rise from the dead (Psalm 16:9–10), and be called Immanuel—which means "God with us" (Isaiah 7:14). Jesus Christ fulfilled these three prophecies and at least three hundred more.[14] When we remember Jesus Christ, let us remember who He truly is. He is the God of the universe, the only one with the power to rise from the dead. He is also a man born into a family, and in His human experience, He drew close to each one of us.

Paul intimately refers to this message of the savior of the universe as *"my gospel"*. The reality that God entered fully into our humanity carries unsearchable meaning for each one of us *personally*.

Pope Saint John Paul II unpacks the mystery of Jesus's incarnation in *Redemptor Hominis*: "For, by his Incarnation, he, the son of God, in a certain way united himself with each man. He worked with human hands, he thought with a human mind. He acted with a human will, and with a human heart he loved. Born of the Virgin Mary, he has truly been made one of us, like to us in all things except sin, he, the Redeemer of man."[15]

2. This means that there is nothing that you experience, except sin, to which your Savior cannot relate. He has entered into your joys and your sorrows. He knows

---

[14] "Biblical Prophecies Fulfilled by Jesus," CBN (15 December, 2023): https://www1.cbn.com/biblestudy/biblical-prophecies-fulfilled-by-jesus.

[15] John Paul II, *Redemptor Hominis*, encyclical letter, Vatican website (15 December, 2023): https://www.vatican.va/content/john-paul-ii/en/encyclicals/documents/hf_jp-ii_enc_04031979_redemptor-hominis.html.

what it is like to wake up and go to work and to be part of a family. He knows what it is like to experience temptation and feel the pain of abandonment and tragedy. He is not indifferent to the details of your life, but rather, He loves you so much that He chose to experience these details—joys, inanities, and sufferings—himself. What does it mean to you that Jesus, fully God, entered into the human experience? How do you experience Immanuel (God-with-us) in your daily life?

3. A. What did Paul say about himself and God's word in 2 Timothy 2:9–10?

It must have been difficult for Paul to sit in a cell when he felt like he was made to spread the gospel far and wide. Yet he knew that despite his chains, the Church would continue to grow.

God invites us to take part in building His kingdom, but it is not mainly up to us. The pressure is off. While God calls us to take part in building His kingdom, we are not the world's savior—God is. We may experience internal and external barriers to spreading the gospel, but God's word cannot and will not be tamed. It will reach hearts, it will change hearts, and in the end, it will bring about salvation.

B. In what ways do you see God's word taking effect in the world and in your life that reveal its power to break barriers? Maybe He broke through to a friend whose heart was hardened to Him. Maybe you witnessed someone draw close to God through suffering. Maybe you are seeing the Holy Spirit do something new in your parish or community. Does it encourage you to persevere in your faith as Paul did? Does this give you hope no matter the state of the world? Why or why not?

Quiet your Heart and enjoy His presence…"With men this is impossible; but with God all things are possible" (Matthew 19:26).

Dear Lord,

Help me to remember that I serve a God of unlimited supply and resources. There are circumstances in my life that I don't know how to resolve. I try to come up with solutions to no avail and easily fall into discouragement. I long to have Paul's perspective. Even as he sat chained in prison, he was able to focus on the fact that the gospel he preached was not in chains. He was able to remember that his limitations did not limit your power. The same is true in my life.

This is the situation that I'm trying to fix [ ].

I hand it over to You.

Please release your power, creativity, and purpose in my life.

I trust You. Please take care of everything. Amen.

Conclusion

Anne-Marie Schmidt grew up in a devout Catholic family in Czechoslovakia. In her talk "To Hell and Back,"[16] she tells the story of her experience going through World War II. When she was a young woman, the Nazis took over her town and sent her to a concentration camp. Anne-Marie's story is filled with incredible recollections. The Gestapo somehow forgot to confiscate her Bible. She nursed a Russian soldier who recognized "the man on the cross" and converted to Christianity as he died. She baptized soldiers who meant her harm. Of all the miracles she mentioned, however, one stood out to me the most. Anne-Marie observed that the priests in her town who had received the Eucharist every day were the ones who stayed faithful to Jesus no matter what. It's clear evidence that the sacraments are a source of strength that helps keep us faithful to Christ. After all, Jesus says, "Abide in me, and I in you. As the branch cannot bear fruit by itself, unless it abides in the vine, neither can you, unless you abide in me" (John 15:4).

---

[16] Anne-Marie Schmidt, "To Hell and Back: Divine Love and the Cross," Lighthouse Media Augustine Institute.

So far, Saint Paul has urged Timothy to rekindle his faith, hold fast to sound doctrine, guard what was entrusted to him, and accept suffering for the gospel. These commands and requests can seem daunting. How can one stay so faithful? Anne-Marie gives us the answer: Stay close to the church.

The beauty of our Catholic faith is that it removes the guesswork from our lives. Yes, our relationships with God are personal and unique, but if we are wondering how to kindle our faith and stay true to what we have been given, the Church has given us the fuel.

Embrace the practices of the Catholic Church. Worship God at Mass. Draw near to Jesus in the Eucharist. Get to know Him in Adoration. Meditate on His life through prayer and the rosary. Receive the witness of His glory by learning about the saints. Receive His unending mercy in confession. Let the church root your entire life in the gospel. When you create the habit of receiving the sacraments and practicing the faith, you integrate the wisdom of the church into your being. It then becomes much easier to safeguard the deposit of faith that has been handed down. Our church, in her teachings, has guarded the Truth and stayed faithful to Christ in every age. Lean in.

Want to learn more about this topic? Don't miss this lesson's short video from Mallory at walkingwithpurpose.com/videos.

My Resolution

In what specific way will I apply what I learned in this lesson?

Examples:

1. I will look for an opportunity this week to step out of my comfort zone and talk about my relationship with God. I'll take the risk of being misunderstood or of a friend thinking I'm weird. I'll remember that no one can argue with my personal experience, and even a little mention of the importance of God in my life can open a window of opportunity for future conversation.

2. When I thought about the metaphor of the athlete needing to compete according to the rules, I was convicted about a specific area of my life where I want God

to bend His rules for me. This is an area of my life where it's hard to obey. I will go to Mass an additional time this week and specifically ask for the grace to surrender this part of my life, trusting that God knows what is best for me.

3. Instead of falling into the pit of self-pity in a specific area of life where I am experiencing suffering, I will spend time each day meditating on the fact that Jesus fully entered into the human experience and suffers with me.

My Resolution:

Catechism Clips

CCC 84 The apostles entrusted the "Sacred deposit" of the faith (the depositum fidei), contained in Sacred Scripture and Tradition, to the whole of the Church. "By adhering to [this heritage] the entire holy people, united to its pastors, remains always faithful to the teaching of the apostles, to the brotherhood, to the breaking of bread and the prayers. So, in maintaining, practicing, and professing the faith that has been handed on, there should be a remarkable harmony between the bishops and the faithful."

CCC 1996 Our justification comes from the grace of God. Grace is favor, the free and undeserved help that God gives us to respond to his call to become children of God, adoptive sons, partakers of the divine nature and of eternal life.

Verse Study

See Appendix 4 for instructions on how to complete a verse study.

1 Corinthians 9:25

1. Verse:

2. Paraphrase:

3. Questions:

4. Cross-references:

5. Personal Application:

 NOTES

 NOTES

Lesson 4

AIM AT RIGHTEOUSNESS

Introduction

"Do your best to present yourself to God as one approved, a workman who has no need to be ashamed, rightly handling the word of truth" (2 Timothy 2:15).

As we move through 2 Timothy, we're continuing to study this passage with two goals in mind. The first is that we want to be growing more like Christ. We're doing this by being discipled ourselves as we allow God's word to read our hearts as much as we read the passages. We're inviting God to reveal ourselves to us—to see the ways in which we are delighting Him with our family resemblance and the ways in which we've got some room to grow.

The second goal we're focusing on is finding tips for ways in which we can pass the faith to the next generation. We want to answer the call to disciple others and we want to do it effectively. Our lesson today gives us instructions for both those goals as we're challenged to aim at righteousness.

If we focus solely on that second goal—seeing how we can pass the faith on—but ignore the first, we're going to find ourselves on a collision course that does not end well. This is because the very generation that we long to see set on fire with love for God has an acute sixth sense that picks up on any hypocrisy or judgment. This means that our words and actions really, really matter.

When we stand before God at the end of our lives, we won't be judged on what others thought about us, the next generation included, but God will be talking to us about how we spoke and acted. We don't want to feel ashamed during that conversation. What we want is for Him to look at us and say, "Well done. I approve. You have no need to be ashamed. You correctly handled the word of truth." We're about to learn how to go about doing that.

What we are longing to pass to the next generation is the greatest treasure. We don't want to wield it like a boulder. We want to present it winsomely, as a precious gift. And if that gift is to seem appealing, it needs to be evident that it's bringing us joy personally. So let's put a smile on our faces, even if we have some troubling thoughts in our minds and unsettled circumstances in our lives. Let's aim at "righteousness, faith, love and peace" (2 Timothy 2:22), for our own sake and that of those around us.

Day One
HE IS FAITHFUL

Read 2 Timothy 2:11–13.

1. In 2 Timothy 2:11–13, Paul continues to unwrap the mystery of Christ's life in us, and ours in Him, in a beautiful and short poem. Write it out in your own words.

2. "If we die with Him, we will also live with Him" (2 Timothy 2:11). The paradox of the gospel message is that if we seek to "save our lives" by living for our own preferences, we will end up serving our passions and will get wrapped up in selfish living. *So counter culture, we live outside the world & a much more satisfying purpose –*

True life is found in dying to self. This means that we lay our preferences and desires at Jesus' feet. We accept the circumstances He gives us. When we do this, He makes us more like Him. We then become capable of Christlike love, joy, and endurance.

How might the Lord be calling you to die with Him in a specific area of your life? Are you being called to die to a particular sin or an insistence on your own way? Has He asked you to allow a dream to die? I promise you, any time God asks us to allow something to die, it is so He can replace it with newness of life. It is always so that our emptiness can then be filled with something better. How could this death lead you to new life in a way that you might not recognize right now?

3. "If we endure, we shall also reign with him" (2 Timothy 2:12).

Romans 5:3–5 gives us insight into the fruit of our suffering: "Suffering produces endurance, and endurance produces character, and character produces hope, and hope does not disappoint us, because God's love has been poured into our hearts through the Holy Spirit who has been given to us."

What might the Lord be calling you to endure right now? In what way can you draw supernatural strength from the Lord as you endure, instead of just gritting your teeth and bearing it?

4. "If we deny him, he also will deny us. If we are faithless, he remains faithful" (2 Timothy 2:12–13). Because God gave us the free will to choose Him or not choose Him, He will honor our choice. If we deny Him, He permits that denial and the consequences that stem from it. God, however, is always faithful in the midst of our faithlessness. His mercy is endless, and He is always waiting to welcome us back with open arms.

Have you ever experienced the consequences of denying God or being faithless? In what ways has He remained faithful to you?

"God's love for our world has opened up a new hope through the death and resurrection of Jesus. And so for those who will take the risk of trusting and following Jesus, God promises vindication and life. For those who reject him, God will honor that decision, and do the same. But people's faithlessness will never compel God to abandon his faithfulness."[17]—Tim Mackie, The Bible Project.

---

[17] Tim Mackie, "Book of 2 Timothy Summary: A Complete Animated Overview," YouTube, The Bible Project (26 November, 2016): https://www.youtube.com/watch?v=urlvnxCaL00&t=396s.

Quiet your heart and enjoy His presence...He remains faithful.

Dear Lord,

Thank you for Your undying faithfulness. From the beginning of creation, You have been faithful to us. When we fell from grace and chose to go our own way, You made a way, and You were faithful. Throughout all of history, You gave us Your presence and were faithful to us. And in Your son Jesus Christ, You gave us, You gave me a redeemer who has always been faithful. Thank you. I know you call me to respond with faithfulness, but that faithfulness comes at a cost that I sometimes think is too high. Lord, give me the grace to say yes to the small thing You put in front of me at this moment. Give me the grace to offer you my life at this moment and to trust that You will give me the grace to offer it to You again in the next. You promise that if I endure the sufferings of this world for the sake of Your name, I will experience Your glory. Yet sometimes those sufferings feel unbearable and meaningless. Give me the faith that believes without seeing and the trust to know that Your word is moving in my life even when I don't perceive it. Amen.

Day Two
SERVING THROUGH RIGHTEOUS ACTIONS

Read 2 Timothy 2:14–15.

1.   A. Yesterday we explored Paul's short hymn about Christ's faithfulness. What was Paul's next instruction to Timothy, according to 2 Timothy 2:14?

The church in Ephesus was excited about following Christ, but they were easily swayed. They were surrounded by false teachers who had different ideas to sell. It was easy to believe the true message of Jesus at one moment and then forget it when a better-sounding argument appeared.

Are we like this? All too often we get excited about our faith and overwhelmed by God's goodness, only to forget everything we know the moment something sounds better or our circumstances change.

B. Think of a specific time in your life when you forgot what you knew about God or began to question His goodness. What was going on? What made you remember Him and reignite trust?

2. A. After Paul told Timothy to remind his people of Christ's faithfulness, he abruptly switched topics. What did he say in the second half of 2 Timothy 2:14?

The church in Ephesus specifically combatted the influence of a group called the Gnostics. Gnosticism was an early church heresy. Its adherents claimed to be Christians but had muddied its teachings by giving long speeches that defended different fantastical theories about God, the world, and the mind and body.[18] These speeches were confusing to those who heard them and encouraged endless debate that took the place of active Christian living. We can easily fall into the same trap. How many of us have sat at the kitchen table debating the world's problems? We may feel great about our ideas, but we have not done a single thing to actually help.

In his book *The 7 Habits of Highly Effective People*, Steven Covey teaches about circles of concern and influence. Covey explains that we have a wide range of concerns, many of which we have no control over. Our circles of influence includes things like our behavior, which in turn influences outcomes in our health, relationships with our children, mood, and situations at work.[19] When people focus their time and energy on their circle of influence, things actually change, and hope is ignited. But idle chatter keeps us in our circles of concern. We talk incessantly about things over which we have no control rather than take action to affect what is in our circle of influence.

B. Are there things that you like to talk about in your circle of concern like fixing other people's problems, obsessing about politics, speculating about the future, or "idle talk" about how other people practice their faith—intense

---

[18] Barclay, 191.

[19] Steven F. Covey, *The 7 Habits of Highly Effective People* (New York: Simon & Schuster, 1989), 34.

conversations that never lead to any kind of real life-change? Write them down.

C. How could you allow those concerns to instead shape concrete actions for positive change?

3. A. Read 2 Timothy 2:15. How did Paul tell Timothy to present himself to God?

The pervasive message of the modern world is that there is no right way to live. While this sounds tolerant on the surface, it results in confusion and pain. Clearly, some choices lead to flourishing, while others lead to misery. Choices that are in harmony with God's will pay off in the end, even if they are costly in the short term.

But it's worth mentioning that we're after God-driven transformation, not human-achieved perfection (self-righteousness). Paul is not encouraging Timothy to claw his way into God's good graces with white-knuckled good behavior but to respond to God's initiation. It is God who draws near, who initiates relationships. It is our job to respond by spending time with Him in prayer, listening to His voice, and acting in obedience to His will.

B. What is the difference between trying to behave our way into God's good graces and falling so deeply in love with Him that we allow His love to change us?

Quiet your heart and enjoy His presence…Let Him be your peace.

Dear Lord,

I place my confidence in You and ask You for Your peace. Father Jacque Philippe compares a soul to the surface of a lake. The more peaceful and tranquil the lake, the more it reflects the sun above it. The more peaceful my soul, the more it will reflect You. And so, I lay before You everything that worries me. I lay before You my anxiety, my negative thoughts, all the things I worry and talk about but have no control over. I offer You the state of the world, the state of my family, my job, my marriage, my children, and [ ]. Bring all these concerns under Your control and guide me on how I should act in each scenario. I give it all to You. Grant me holy desires that lead me to holy actions. And I ask for freedom from idle and speculative thoughts that lead nowhere. You promised that in this world we would have trouble, but then You said that You have overcome the world. I easily forget this. Help me to remember it and to place all my confidence in You. Amen.

Day Three
GUARD AGAINST HERESY

Read 2 Timothy 2:16–18.

1. A. How did Paul describe people who habitually participate in idle talk, and to what did he compare their teaching, according to 2 Timothy 2:16–17?

Paul's use of the word *gangrene* offers us a powerful and unpleasant image. Gangrene is so destructive that it can kill someone in only forty-eight hours. According to Paul, idle and profane talk possesses the same qualities. It attacks and devastates us personally when we fail to control our speech and eats away at the health of our communities.

While all careless talk has destructive power, in this instance, Paul is speaking specifically about teachings that sound like the gospel but are in fact contrary to it. We refer to these kinds of teachings as heresy, an adherence to a religious opinion contrary to Catholic dogma.[20] The ancient world was full of them.

B. Paul described one of these heresies in the second half of 2 Timothy 2:18. What was it and who was spreading it?

---

[20] Heresy, "Definition of Heresy," Oxford Languages (17 December, 2022): https://languages.oup.com/google-dictionary-en/.

57

C. Read *CCC* 989–991. What does the Church teach about our resurrection from the dead? How long has this teaching been around?

2. We have our own heresies to contend with today. We swim in a culture that offers us nice-sounding "truths" that spread like gangrene, leading well-intentioned people away from God. Let's look at a few of those heresies and seek the wisdom of God to find the truth.

What does the Bible say about the following messages:

A. Claim: If you follow Jesus Christ, you will achieve a life filled with health and wealth, void of suffering and sacrifice.

Is this what Christ promised? What did Jesus say in John 16:33?

B. Claim: It doesn't matter what you believe, as long as you believe in something. All religions lead to God; it's just a different path.

Does God agree? See Psalm 96:4–5 and John 14:6.

C. Claim: Do what you want as long as it makes you happy, helps you feel good, and doesn't hurt anybody else.

What insight do we gain from James 1:14–15 and Jeremiah 17:9?

D. Claim: Sin is an outdated idea. Most people are basically good, and religion is just a framework for "being a good person."

How did John describe those who say they have no sin, according to 1 John 1:8?

E. Claim: The world and its events can be distilled down to power struggles between oppressors and the oppressed. We can reach Utopia if only we can achieve complete equality between rich and poor, owner and worker, and different races.

only through Christ — original sin

Does God see the world only from the perspective of the powerful and the powerless? See Galatians 3:27–29. How did Jesus respond to the power dynamics in the world? See Philippians 2:5–8.

3. A. Consider the modern-day heresies above. How do you see them affecting society? How do you see them affecting the Church?

B. Has one of these heresies infiltrated your worldview or the way you live out your faith? If so, which one? Where is the truth in the heresy? Where is the lie?

Quiet your heart and enjoy His presence…He holds you in the palm of His hand.

Dear Lord,

James 3:3–5 compares the tongue to a small rudder that can steer a ship, or a bit that can lead a horse in any direction. The tongue, though small, can change our direction. I come to You and ask for the gift of self-control so that I might gain mastery over my speech and I ask for Your wisdom, with which I can discern and share Your truth. It is so easy to become lazy in my speech and so easy to believe anything that sounds good and helps me get along. And there is also the fact that I don't understand all of Your teachings. Sometimes these heresies, even when I have thought them through, seem to make more sense than the truth put forward in the gospel. Open my eyes and help me to pinpoint the places in which I have developed my opinions based on the spirit of the age instead of Your timeless wisdom.

It can feel overwhelming to remain on the raft of truth while being battered in a sea of lies. But for You, Lord, nothing is difficult. You can do this work in my life, and I put my trust in You to do so. Thank you for loving me enough to protect me in the walls of Your Church. Keep my direction facing You always. Amen.

Day Four
GIFTED FOR HIS GLORY

Read 2 Timothy 2:19–21.

1. A. What hope did Paul offer to Timothy in 2 Timothy 2:19?

    B. Theologians claim that Paul was referring to the Church when he spoke of God's foundation. How does He describe the church in 1 Timothy 3:15?

CCC 769 reminds us, "The Church, and through her the world, will not be perfected in glory without great trials." But throughout her trials, she is always faced toward God, leading her members closer to Him.

Do you struggle to know what is true? Ask the Lord to infuse you with His wisdom and guidance. Trust His Church and lean into her teachings. This will ensure that even as you stumble on your way to Him, you are facing in the right direction.

2. A. What did Paul describe in 2 Timothy 2:20?

It would be easy to look at this verse and conclude that some people have gifts and talents that are more special to God than others, but Paul is not making that distinction. Each of us has different gifts and talents, and while the world may value some more than others, God does not operate as the world does. He looks at the heart (1 Samuel 16:7).

St. Thérèse of Lisieux compared our unique humanity to the different flowers in a field and wrote, "I saw that every flower He has created has a beauty of its own, that the splendor of the rose and the lily's whiteness do not deprive the violet of its scent nor make less ravishing the daisy's charm. I saw that if every little flower wished to be a rose, Nature would lose her spring adornments, and the fields would no longer be enameled with their varied flowers. So it is in the world of souls, the living garden of the Lord. It pleases Him to create great Saints, who may be compared with the lilies or the rose, but He has also created little ones, who must be content to be daisies or violets, nestling at His feet to delight His eyes when He should choose to look at them...Our Lord's love shines out just as much through a little soul that yields completely to His grace as in the greatest...what delights Him is the simplicity of these flowers of the field and by stooping low, He shows how infinitely great He is."[21]

Each flower is different yet precious to God, and so it is with His people. God created you with a purpose that only you can fill. He gave you gifts and talents that are just as important to Him as the gifts and talents of the person to whom you compare yourself. The matter is not of rank, but willing service. If you are willing to lay yourself at God's feet, He will use you powerfully for his glory.

B. What are you good at? How do you enjoy helping others? What do you think of these things? Do you see them as valuable to God? Why or why not? Write a short prayer, thanking God for these things, and offer them in service to Him.

3. According to 2 Timothy 2:21, who will become ready for special use, just like the utensils in the house?

[21] Saint Therese of Lisieux, *Story of a Soul* (Charlotte, North Carolina:Tan Books, 2010) 4.

Quiet your heart and enjoy His presence…Let Him fill you with all you need.

Dear Lord,

I echo the words of the psalmist when he wrote: "For a day in thy courts is better than a thousand elsewhere. I would rather be a doorkeeper in the house of my God than dwell in the tents of wickedness" (Psalm 84:10). I long to be a vessel for You—emptied of self-interest, conceit, judgmental attitudes, worries—and filled with the sweet presence of Your Holy Spirit. I lift my heart to You—throw open wide the doors—and invite You in. Soak me in Your goodness. Make an imprint of Your character in my inmost being so that I may reflect Your love to all I encounter today. Amen.

Day Five
PURSUE GREATNESS

Read 2 Timothy 2:22–26.

1. What did Paul tell Timothy to shun, and what did he tell him to pursue, according to 2 Timothy 2: 22–23?

2. A. What did Paul tell Timothy to avoid in 2 Timothy 2:23–24? What did he tell Timothy to do instead?

Years ago, I sat in spiritual direction and told the priest before me all the mud and the muck that was going on at my place of work. Part of me was seeking advice, and part of me was venting, trying to make myself look better than my coworkers. Once I finished, the wise priest looked at me and said, "You know, I believe you could be a great lady. You could rise above all this junk and live at a higher level. But you aren't there yet."

I am so grateful for that priest's honest words. He had the courage to call me to the same standard Paul set for Timothy, to rise about the stupid and senseless controversies and to leave behind the quarrels. He motivated me to pursue greatness instead of settling for pettiness.

    B. Can you think of a specific example of a time you got wrapped up in a controversy or quarrel? What was it? What drew you in? How could you have avoided it and practiced kindness?

3.   A. How should the Lord's servant act according to 2 Timothy 2:24 and the first half of verse 25?

    B. Can you think of a time when someone corrected you harshly? What about a time when someone corrected you gently? What was the difference in your experience? What can you learn from these two different scenarios when dealing with others?

4.   What did Paul say may be the result of Christian kindness, patience, and gentleness in the lives of others, according to 2 Timothy 2: 25–26?

Romans 2:4 reminds us that it is God's kindness that leads to repentance. We can apply this to our own interactions with people who are walking away from God. Showing kindness doesn't mean applauding and agreeing with sin or throwing truth out of the window. But it means speaking with gentleness, humbly acknowledging that we don't have all the facts, and recognizing that we, too, fall short of what God asks of us. What if we were the ones whose kindness made those around us want to open the door of their heart just a bit to let God's merciful grace rush in? What might change if we became the soft place for people to land in their brokenness?

Quiet your heart and enjoy His presence…Let His kindness draw you in.

Dear Lord,

When I look in the mirror, I see what is ordinary in me, what is not as good as other people. I see a woman who cannot possibly live up to all that life demands. I look at to-do lists with barely anything crossed off. I look at pictures of other people's lives and compare myself to their looks, their kids, their jobs, their husbands, their houses, their vacations, their money…and the list goes on. I renounce the lie that I am only as good as the world says I am. I accept the truth that You delight in me and have created me for a special purpose in Your kingdom. I accept the truth that when You see me, You see a flower in a field that brings You joy. You see me as a gift to the world, and You have given me everything I need to glorify You in this life. Help me to accept this truth. Help me stake my claim on this truth and reject any lie that might get in the way. Thank you for Your creativity and for expressing it through me. Lord, I also lay before You all the ways that I refuse to leave behind my youthful passions. I know that I am a work in progress and I ask You to help me to progress into maturity. I know that I can become a great lady in Your good time. I take hope in that, and I give You permission to do everything You need to bring me into full maturity marked by righteousness, kindness, temperance, and selflessness. I love You, Lord; help me to love You more. Amen.

Conclusion

I used to work in catering at the LSU alumni hotel. I usually served at events in the hotel, but one day I walked in for my shift and learned that I would be driving across town to cater an in-home event.

I got in my car, drove across town, down a lonely road, and arrived at the home of an oil tycoon. This man had invented a valve for the oil industry that made him a billionaire, and his home boldly displayed wealth. There was a ton of gold, fine large paintings, and rugs worth more than my college tuition.

As I drove away, I had a hearty laugh over the whole experience. It was so out of the blue! The house was far beyond anything I had seen, but then again, what did I expect? Our homes reflect who we are.

In 2 Timothy 2:20–21, Paul compared us to the items in a home. As members of the church, we are part of God's family. And as part of God's family, He comes and makes His home in us. Are we brave enough to allow God to make us into a home that accurately reflects who He is? What will it take?

Some homes must be stripped bare and rebuilt from the ground up to reflect the owner's preferences. Others need tune-ups, patched-up holes, and fixed pipes. In fact, the more extensive the needed work is, the more admiration it draws from those who see it completed. The remodeling might cause pain, but the end product is always worth it.

Biblical scholar David Guzick speculates from Paul's writings to Timothy that Timothy was an ordinary man of ordinary courage, called to an extraordinary task that required tremendous courage. For Timothy to fulfill his call to accurately reflect God to the Church in Ephesus, God had to do some divine renovating in Timothy's heart.

C. S. Lewis spoke of such a renovation in *Mere Christianity*:[22]

> Imagine yourself as a living house. God comes in to rebuild that house. At first, perhaps, you can understand what He is doing. He is getting the drains right and stopping the leaks in the roof and so on; you knew that those jobs needed doing and so you are not surprised. But presently He starts knocking the house about in a way that hurts abominably and does not seem to make any sense. What on earth is He up to? The explanation is that He is building quite a different house from the one you thought of—throwing out a new wing here, putting on an extra floor there, running up towers, making courtyards. You thought you were being made into a decent little cottage: but He is building a palace. He intends to come and live in it Himself.

What does God need to remodel in your heart so you can boldly reflect His personality? What beliefs need reforming? Are there behaviors and passions over which you have no control? Let Him in. Let Him do the remodeling so that your life reveals who He is to all who come in contact with you.

Want to learn more about this topic? Don't miss this lesson's short video from Mallory at walkingwithpurpose.com/videos.

---

[22] C.S. Lewis, *Mere Christianity* (United Kingdom: HarperCollins, 2001), 204.

My Resolution

In what specific way will I apply what I learned in this lesson?

Examples:

1. I will share the difference that Jesus has made in my life with three people. I will also ask them to share their story with me and listen for ways I can learn from them.

2. I will pay attention to the messages that I am receiving during the day and examine the truth that they convey. I will measure what they are telling me against what I know about the gospel so I can decide whether these messages would lead me closer to Christ or farther from Him.

3. I will write down three phrases that can help me to guard myself against idle chatter in conversation. I will practice those phrases, such as "You know, she probably has a side to this story that she isn't here to share, so let's wait for her to be here to talk about it" or "It does seem like there is so much to be worried about in the world, but I always remind myself that there is always some sort of light in the darkness" and then use them in my conversations.

My Resolution:

Catechism Clips

CCC 989 We firmly believe, and hence we hope that, just as Christ is truly risen from the dead and lives forever, so after death the righteous will live forever with the risen Christ, and he will raise them up on the last day. Our resurrection, like his own, will be the work of the Most Holy Trinity: "If the Spirit of him who raised Jesus from the dead dwells in you, he who raised Christ Jesus from the dead will give life to your mortal bodies also through His Spirit who dwells in you."

CCC 990 The term "flesh" refers to man in his state of weakness and mortality. The "resurrection of the flesh" (the literal formulation of the Apostles' Creed) means not only that the immortal soul will live on after death, but that even our "mortal body" will come to life again.

CCC 991 Belief in the resurrection of the dead has been an essential element of the Christian faith from its beginnings. "The confidence of Christians is the resurrection of the dead; believing this we live." "How can some of you say that there is no resurrection of the dead? But if there is no resurrection of the dead, then Christ has not been raised; if Christ has not been raised, then our preaching is in vain and your faith is in vain…But in fact Christ has been raised from the dead, the first fruits of those who have fallen asleep."

Verse Study

See Appendix 4 for instructions on how to complete a verse study.

Acts 1:8

1. Verse:

2. Paraphrase:

3. Questions:

4. Cross-references:

5. Personal Application:

NOTES

NOTES

Lesson 5: Connect Coffee Talk

THESE LAST DAYS

You can view this talk via the accompanying DVD or digital download purchase, or access it online at walkingwithpurpose.com/videos.

"But understand this, that in the last days there will come times of stress. For men will be lovers of self, lovers of money, proud, arrogant, abusive, disobedient to their parents, ungrateful, unholy, inhuman, implacable, slanderers, profligates, fierce, haters of good, treacherous, reckless, swollen with conceit, lovers of pleasure rather than lovers of God, holding the form of religion but denying the power of it. Avoid such people. For among them are those who make their way into households and capture weak women, burdened with sins and swayed by various impulses, who will listen to anybody and can never arrive at a knowledge of the truth." 2 Timothy 3:1–7

I. Effects of a Utopian Worldview

   A. On Politics

   B. On Psychology

   C. On Education and Parenting

II. Capturing a Better Vision

"Man cannot live without love. He remains a being that is incomprehensible for himself, his life is senseless, if love is not revealed to him, if he does not encounter love, if he does not experience it and make it his own, if he does not participate intimately in it. This, as has already been said, is why Christ the Redeemer 'fully reveals man to himself.'

The man who wishes to understand himself thoroughly—and not just in accordance with immediate, partial, often superficial, and even illusory standards and measures of his being—he must with his unrest, uncertainty and even his weakness and sinfulness, with his life and death, draw near to Christ. He must, so to speak, enter into him with all his own self, he must 'appropriate' and assimilate the whole of the reality of the Incarnation and Redemption in order to find himself. If this profound process takes place within him, he then bears fruit not only of adoration of God but also of deep wonder at himself."—Saint John Paul II[23]

Questions for Discussion

1. Do you see evidence of a utopian view of the world around you? In what way?

2. Do you agree with Saint John Paul II when he says, "Man cannot live without love. He remains a being that is incomprehensible for himself, his life is senseless, if love is not revealed to him"? Why or why not?

3. Saint John Paul II went on to write that a person needs to enter into Christ wholeheartedly in order to find himself. Then he made an incredible claim: "If this profound process takes place within him, he then bears fruit not only of adoration of God but also of deep wonder at himself."[24] Why might closer union with God, and adoration of Him, bring us to a place of greater self-acceptance and wonder?

---

[23] John Paul II, *Redemptor Hominis*, encyclical letter, Vatican website (15 December, 2023): https://www.vatican.va/content/john-paul-ii/en/encyclicals/documents/hf_jp-ii_enc_04031979_redemptor-hominis.html.

[24] John Paul II, *Redemptor Hominis*, encyclical letter, Vatican website (15 December, 2023): https://www.vatican.va/content/john- paul-ii/en/encyclicals/documents/hf_jp-ii_enc_04031979_redemptor-hominis.html.

 NOTES

Lesson 6

ALERT TO YOUR SURROUNDINGS

Introduction

How should we live out the Christian faith in our specific circumstances, places, and times? In this third chapter of 2 Timothy, Paul sought to answer these questions. Broadening the scope of his letter, he addressed the external challenges of preaching the gospel and shepherding a church in the middle of a sin-ridden world. If Timothy was going to fulfill his ministry in the church at Ephesus, he needed to be able to diagnose the unique problems that he faced, guard himself against those threats, and hear God's direction on how to bring the gospel into this unique environment.

This is an excellent way for us to follow today as we seek to make disciples and bring the beauty of the gospel to the next generation. Father John Riccardo recently spoke about this blueprint, giving simple language and practical steps on how to diagnose problems in our communities and follow God's plan for addressing them.

He said that revival in the Church will not come from excellent brainstorming sessions, implementing best practices, or brilliant man-made strategies.[25] While those things can be good and helpful, our communities will become vibrant when we go to God first, ask Him to reveal His plan for them, and then implement His plan.

The answer—the revival—will come from relying on God as the source of transformation and power, not simply our own efforts and plans. How can we hear His voice and seek His direction? Father Riccardo suggested three questions to ask God in prayer.

---

[25] Father John Riccardo, "Restoring the Initiative to God," *You Were Born for This with Fr. John and Mary*, podcast audio (16 January, 2023): https://podcasts.apple.com/us/podcast/episode-212-restoring-the-initiative-to-god/id1492145319?i=1000594666144Podcast

What is really happening here?

If we are going to know how to proceed with an issue in our life or help someone in theirs, we have to learn what God wants us to address. Where there is sin, there is a wound, and while we might have a good idea of what that wound is, God is the only one who can give us a complete understanding of what is wounding a specific heart or community. God must reveal it for us to understand the problem in front of us.

What is the enemy's strategy?

Similar to the military, we can have the best plan in the world, but the enemy also has a plan. In this case, we know the devil doesn't win, but he does get a vote, and his goal is to decimate as many souls as possible between now and God's final victory. We will be much more effective for God's cause if we sit before Him and let Him show us the other side's strategy.

What are You asking me to do?

If God has revealed the wound and the enemy's destructive strategy, He can now reveal what He wants us to do based on the answers to the first two questions.

Having sat in prayer and listening to God's voice, you can be sure (to the best of your ability) that you are following what He wants, and you will see the difference. You will experience breakthroughs in your faith, a new level of peace in suffering, and increased confidence when sharing the good news of Christ.

As you pray through this week's lessons, keep these three questions in mind. Throughout this lesson, you will witness Paul answer each of these questions for Timothy. The world might live one way, but Timothy was to live differently.

This week, I invite you to make it personal. As you see Paul instruct Timothy, ask God to speak to you. Ask Him to reveal the wounds in your own heart and community. Ask Him to reveal the enemy's strategies against you and those you love. Ask Him to show you what to do to draw closer to Him and draw others to Him. As He answers you, take some time to journal so you can follow in obedience and witness God do the work.

Day One
ENGAGING THE TIMES

Read 2 Timothy 3:1–5.

1. A. What did Paul want Timothy to understand according to 2 Timothy 3:1?

   B. Scriptures that describe *the last days* or *the end of the age* easily lead to confusion and speculation about the second coming of Christ. Does anyone know the timing of Christ's second coming? See Matthew 24:36.

2. A. Although no one knows exactly when the very end of days and Christ's second coming will occur, the Catholic Church has defined the time in which we live. In what age are we living according to *CCC* 670? When did this age begin?

Paul wrote to Timothy with the conviction that Christ was coming back within a generation. But according to the Church's definition of *the last age*, he lived in it, and so do we.

   B. Knowing that we are living in the final age of the world but that we cannot know the time of Christ's second coming, how should we respond to this cultural moment, according to Matthew 24:42–44?

We can stay awake and be ready to engage our culture in two ways. First, we draw near to God. We stake our claim in His truth so that we can withstand the devil's deceptive tactics. Second, we engage our culture with the truth and joy of Jesus Christ so that He can use us as a vessel to bring as many people to Him as possible.

C. In what ways do you "stay awake"? In what ways might you be "asleep" and unprepared to live and share the gospel in today's culture?

3. In 2 Timothy 3:1, Paul describes the last days as distressing, but he does not elaborate by describing catastrophic events as Jesus did (Matthew 24:3–31). Instead, he lists behaviors and distortions that flow from the hearts of men, that would signify the end times. List the behaviors mentioned in 2 Timothy 3:2–3.

The word *narcissism* stems from the Greek myth about Narcissus. Narcissus was to live to old age only if he failed to recognize himself. Eventually, he saw his reflection in a river. He fell so deeply in love with himself that he refused to stop staring at himself in the water. His refusal to love something other than himself eventually led to his death as he wasted away gazing at his reflection.

We were created to focus our love, worship, and honor on God, and the more we do, the more we become who we were meant to be. We are to love ourselves, but not in a self-congratulatory way. Our love of self should be rooted in an appreciation for all that God has made and the goodness He bestows on His creation and creatures.

Quiet your heart and enjoy His presence…Invite Him to help you grow in humility.

Litany of Humility
That others may be loved more than I,
Jesus, grant me the grace to desire it.
That others may be esteemed more than I,
Jesus, grant me the grace to desire it.
That, in the opinion of the world, others may increase and I may decrease,
Jesus, grant me the grace to desire it.
That others may be chosen and I set aside,
Jesus, grant me the grace to desire it.
That others may be praised and I go unnoticed,
Jesus, grant me the grace to desire it.
That others may be preferred to me in everything,
Jesus, grant me the grace to desire it.

That others may become holier than I, provided that I may become as holy as I should,
Jesus, grant me the grace to desire it.[26]
Amen.

Day Two
MORE SIN, MORE GRACE

Reread 2 Timothy 3:1–5.

1. A. How do you think the sins mentioned by Paul in 2 Timothy 3:2–3 find their root in the sin of self-love?

    B. Which sins do you see affecting our current society most? How?

    C. Which ones do you see in yourself?

It would be easy for us to allow these verses to lead us into despair either because we are burdened by the idea of a society that has no regard for God and His laws, or because we see these behaviors in ourselves and have not been able to root them out. But take heart—these verses are not here to lead us into discouragement. The *Catechism of the Catholic Church* does tell us that the present time is marked by "distress" (*CCC* 672). But it is also a time of great hope.

2. A. Evil will increase in the last days. What else will also increase, according to Acts 2:17?

---

[26] Rafael Cardinal Merry del Val y Zulueta, "Litany of Humlity," EWTN (5 May, 2023): https://www.ewtn.com/catholicism/devotions/litany-of-humility-245.

B.   Read Romans 5:20–21. As sin increases, what else increases?

We can read the signs of the times with hardened hearts and despairing attitudes. We can be careless, giving ourselves over to temptation, and fall into the traps meant to steal, kill, and destroy. Or we can surrender to God and ask Him to pour out His spirit in our lives. How compelling it is when those of us formerly enslaved by our sin step into freedom. As living proof of what God can do with a life surrendered to Him, we can invite others out of a culture plagued by death and into a culture of God's new life.

3.   God made you for this time and place. In what parts of your life do you most engage with the culture? Maybe it's in your job or your kids' activities. Maybe you have hobbies or frequent certain social scenes in which few people know about Jesus or are interested in following Him. How can you enter into those situations and invite others into the culture of light, led by the Holy Spirit?

"Christ needs you to enlighten the world and to show it the 'path to life.' The challenge is to make the Church's 'yes' to Life concrete and effective. The struggle will be long, and it needs each one of you. Place your intelligence, your talents, your enthusiasm, your compassion and your fortitude at the service of life!"—Pope Saint John Paul II

Quiet your heart and enjoy His presence…In Him there is no darkness.

Dear Lord,

You have made me for this time and place on purpose, and You have given me everything I need to be alert and ready. It is easy for me to look at the world, compare it to the behaviors Paul described, and see only the enemy on the move. How easy it is to lose heart. How easy it is to want to wash my hands of our society and retreat from the fight. But the truth is that You call me to be a person of hope. You call me to engage the culture. You call me to stand firm on Your team, for Your heavenly cause, and to use my story with all my faults and failures to show others the way to You. Give me the grace to answer Your call with hope and confidence, Lord God. I offer You my intelligence. Teach me to use it to tell others of Your goodness in a compelling and inviting way. I offer You my talents to display Your glory in places that need to see it. I offer You my enthusiasm, my compassion, and my perseverance, Lord, all for the sake of Your kingdom. Amen.

Day Three
REJECTING EMPTY RELIGION

Reread 2 Timothy 3:1–5.

1. Today we continue to read Paul's list of behaviors that will increase in frequency and intensity in the last days. Which ones did he list in 2 Timothy 3:4?

2. Paul ended this verse saying that people will be lovers of pleasure instead of lovers of God. Paul described lovers of pleasure as enemies of Christ in his letter to the Philippians. What did he say about them according to Philippians 3:18–19?

3. A. How does someone act when they live for the love of pleasure? How does someone act when they live for the love of God? What are the differences?

    B. What pleasures are you prone to serve to excess (examples: food, drink, sex, substance abuse, excessive shopping, or personal comfort)? What might God want to offer that is better than those things?

4. A. Most of us struggle back and forth between being lovers of pleasure and lovers of God. God created the earth and all that is in it. God's creation is good. It is beautiful. It reflects Him. Just as He gave us Himself, He gave us His stuff to enjoy. The key is to keep it all in proper order. What insight can we gain from 1 Corinthians 10:31 about how to do this?

B. What is the difference between allowing created things to lead us into worship and allowing created things to become what we worship?

5. A. What is the last sinful trait in Paul's list, according to 2 Timothy 3:5?

God does not want us to follow His rules so that we can appear to be religious while we secretly give our hearts to other things. Instead, He desires that we fall in love with Him and let our faithfulness to Him flow out of that love. Genuine faith and true love for God is the only faith that has the power to transform.

B. How do you engage in this battle in your own heart?

Quiet your heart and enjoy His presence…Let His love change you.

"When I look at your heavens, the work of your fingers, the moon and the stars that you have established; what are human beings that you are mindful of, mortals that you care for them? Yet you have made them a little lower than God, and crowned them with glory and honor." Psalm 8:3–5

Dear Lord,

It can be so easy to turn my faith into a checklist. How quickly I can go from sitting before You with heartfelt prayer to sitting before You just to mark something off a to-do list as I go to chase my worldly dreams and ambition. Help me to realize that not only is my faith empty if You don't fill it, but everything else is as well. You are the being that reveals life's meaning, life's goodness, life's joy. You are the One who shows me who I am, that I am not enough on my own, but in Your arms You make me all I was created to be and more. I know all these things, Lord, and I still turn to my idols without a good reason. So I submit them to You again. I submit to You all that threatens to lure my affections away from You and render my faith empty and powerless. I especially give You my attachment to [ ]. In its/their place, Lord, please fill me with Your Holy Spirit. Show me Your presence and power. Make me firm in hope and strong in grace. Transform me from the inside out so people would see that faith can be genuine and that a life lived for God is the best kind of life there is. Amen.

Day Four
STRENGTHENING OUR MINDS

Read 2 Timothy 3:1–7.

Today we dive into verses that may make us want to stop learning and start defending. Let us resolve here at the outset to resist this temptation and instead glean all the wisdom we can.

1. In 2 Timothy 3:5, Paul told Timothy to avoid people who exhibited the kind of behavior he listed. What does Paul say they were doing in church communities according to 2 Timothy 3:6? Who were they targeting?

It is important to note that Paul is not singling out women as the only ones who could be weighed down by sins and desires. Throughout his writings, and even in 2 Timothy, Paul calls out men by name who exhibit problematic behaviors and beliefs. Paul spoke specifically about women in this instance because these men were exclusively targeting the women of the community.

2. A. Read Ephesians 4:14–15. How does Paul describe those who are like spiritual children or are spiritually immature, according to Ephesians 4:14?

These verses are a gift to us, a challenge to take a long, hard look in the mirror and identify where we still easily succumb to the wind of every doctrine, conspiracy, plot, or scheme. These verses are an invitation to pursue maturity.

So, what does it look like to be a spiritually *mature* woman? A spiritually mature woman lives out of an identity rooted in who God says she is. She has an active prayer life and sacramental life. She lives with the intention of conforming her behavior in obedience to God and repents when she fails. She tests the messages and beliefs she receives against what she knows to be true about the gospel. She receives corrections and makes changes in her life when she goes off track. She lives her entire life with God at the center and teaches others to do the same in her friendships.

B. Which habits have helped you grow into spiritual maturity, holding fast to Christ? Which habits help you withstand the "winds and the waves" of our culture?

3. A. How else did Paul describe these women in 2 Timothy 3:7?

In this verse, Paul described the concept of a "spiritual consumer." A spiritual consumer is someone who consumes what the Church offers but does not change how she lives and never steps up to give what she has received. The woman who "always desires instruction but never arrives at knowledge of the truth" might be a woman who seeks teaching especially because she seeks *novelty*. Because she seeks novelty, she's always after the latest "spiritual thing." This makes her susceptible to fads in religion rather than fortitude in faith. God can "hook us" by our desire for spiritual novelty, but He desires maturity for us.

The "spiritual consumer" goes to Mass week after week, hears the sermons, and receives the Eucharist but never conforms her will to God's. She may go to Bible study for years, consume instruction, and feel great about her small group but never fully implement the instruction into her life. The spiritual consumer is not the same as the spiritually needy—those who are in need of care and nourishment in a time of vulnerability. After a season of being served, she never transitions to serving, taking on the responsibility to pass on what she has received to other women. She enjoys the teachings of Jesus but is less interested in picking up her cross and following Him daily.

B. Have there been times when you'd describe yourself as a "spiritual consumer"? If so, in what way?

Quiet your heart and enjoy His presence…May He make you a conduit of blessing.

Dear Lord,

I know that You desire that I get joy out of participating in the life of the Church. As I step out to serve, I know I need to continue to fill my heart with your goodness through prayer, study, community, and the sacraments. I cannot give what I don't have. That being said, I know that You don't bless me so that I hoard the blessing but that I become the blessing. Help me to arrive at the truth, root myself in it, and offer it to others as I continue to grow. Amen.

Day Five
AN ENLIGHTENED MIND AND AUTHENTIC FAITH

Read 2 Timothy 3:8–9.

1. A. Read 2 Timothy 3:8–9. To whom did Paul compare these deceitful people? Does Paul believe that these people will triumph?

In Exodus 7:8–10, Moses and his brother Aaron performed a miracle for Pharaoh. Aaron threw down his staff and it turned into a snake. Pharaoh called his magicians, whose names, according to Jewish tradition, were Jan'nes and Jam'bres. They followed suit and their staffs also turned into snakes. Aaron's snake ate the others. All who watched saw that the God of Moses and Aaron was far superior to the false gods of the Jannes and Jambres.

   B. What insight do we gain from 1 John 4:4 that should give us hope in the face of evil?

No matter how dark the darkness feels, no matter how deceitful the evil one, we know that in the end, God wins. Truth will eventually triumph and the lies will be exposed for what they are.

2. How were the men who opposed the truth and negatively influenced women described in 2 Timothy 3:8?

3. A. What do you think is the opposite of a corrupt mind? See Romans 12:2 and Ephesians 1:18 for insight.

   B. How can you cultivate a renewed, enlightened intellect in your own life?

4. A. What are some words that describe the opposite of counterfeit faith?

   B. What is one way 1 Peter 1:6–7 says that genuine faith is cultivated?

   C. Is there any area of our life where your faith is being tested by suffering? Are you being asked to have faith in God's timing or God's plan? Has anything in particular encouraged you as you endeavor to allow the suffering to refine your faith?

Quiet your heart and enjoy His presence...He will finish what He started in you.

Dear Lord,

Sometimes the Christian life seems more like a giant to-do list—endless ways to get better rather than an invitation to sit at Your feet. Help me to reject the lie that perfection is the goal and remember that my one job is to stay close to You. You have a much better idea of the person You made me to be than I do, and it is in my surrender to You that You will bring that woman to the light. There are many ways in which I have embraced a form of spiritual immaturity because it is easier to remain where I am than to allow you to lead me farther down the path to You. How do You want me to grow intellectually? How do You want me to grow in authentic faith? What do You want me to do?

I give You permission to flood me with the grace I need to lay down my desire to be served and comforted so that You develop me in the most beautiful of ways. Whatever you ask, however You want me to mature, I say yes to You before I can talk myself out of it. I take comfort in the fact that You know whom you are working with! You know all that is broken in me, yet You come into my heart and fuse me together like a stained-glass window, broken, mended by You, showing Your glory and Your story to the world. Thank you for Your patience with me, Lord, and help me to take confidence in the fact that You will finish the work You started. My only job is to respond to Your initiation and draw closer to You. Amen.

Conclusion

Jonathan Isaac was a rising star in the NBA. With making millions, ever-increasing career status, and a lifestyle of fame and money, he seemed to have everything. Underneath the facade of worldly gain, however, he suffered debilitating anxiety and panic attacks that were increasing in frequency.

Isaac had given his life to Christ years before. He identified as a Christian, but it was clear to him and others that he was not living like one.

Terrified by his anxiety, Isaac reluctantly accepted a teammate's invitation to go to chapel before one of his games. The preacher opened up the scriptures and read Luke 6:46, "Why do you call me 'Lord, Lord,' and do not do what I tell you?" Isaac was cut to the heart, disoriented by what he heard. He had never heard that scripture before but saw himself in the words. He regularly called upon the Lord but rarely chose to live as He commanded. Hearing this scripture verse eventually led him to a powerful conversion. Today, he tries to live every moment for God no matter what it might cost him.

Hebrews 4:12 tells us, "For the word of God is living and active, sharper than any two-edged sword, piercing to the division of soul and spirit, of joints and marrow, and discerning the thoughts and intentions of the heart." The scriptures pierced Jonathan Isaac's heart when they revealed his duplicity and challenged him to change course. And the more time we spend in the Bible, the more we experience God's conviction and call to transformation.

The words in the pages of our Bibles were God-breathed when they were written, and they are God-breathed when we read them. These living words have the power of the Holy Spirit to bring someone out of darkness and into the light. They have the power to reveal our sins and inspire us to give God our heart of stone and accept from Him a heart of flesh. They have the power to bring us out of despair and into hope.

It's no mistake that Paul ends this section of his letter by telling Timothy to stay rooted in the scriptures. In Ephesians 6:13, Paul tells us, "Therefore take up the whole armor of God, so that you may be able to withstand that evil day, and having done everything, to stand firm." He then listed out five elements of the armor of God. All of them are defensive except for the sword of the Spirit, the Word of God. God has given us everything we need to draw near Him and fight the evil that Paul mentioned during this lesson. The more we root ourselves in His word, the more we look like Jesus and are better prepared for the battle ahead.

Want to learn more about this topic? Don't miss this lesson's short video from Mallory at walkingwithpurpose.com/videos.

My Resolution

In what specific way will I apply what I learned in this lesson?

Examples:

1. I will think of a situation in my life in which I really need to know God's plan. I will engage in three half-hour prayer sessions. At first I will ask God: Where is the wound? In the second, I will ask God: What is the enemy's strategy? And in the third I will ask: What do you want me to do? I will then commit to doing what He asks.

2. I will take the following self-reflection based on material from day 2 to the chapel and journal with it: What qualities of spiritual *maturity* do I see in myself? Give thanks for this development. Where do I exhibit traits of spiritual *immaturity*?

Why am I holding on to spiritual immaturity? I will then ask the Lord where He wants me to arrive at truth, root myself in it, and become a blessing to others in my community. I will then write it down and do one thing to take a step forward in spiritual maturity and service.

3. I will commit to spending twenty more minutes a week in the scriptures than I do now. I will also write down verses worth memorizing so I will have them on hand to battle anything that might come my way.

My Resolution:

Catechism Clips

CCC 670 Since the Ascension, God's plan has entered into its fulfillment. We are already at "the last hour." "Already the final age of the world is with us, and the renewal of the world is irrevocably under way; it is even now anticipated in a certain real way, for the Church on earth is endowed already with a sanctity that is real but imperfect." Christ's kingdom already manifests its presence through the miraculous signs that attend its proclamation by the Church.

Verse Study

See Appendix 4 for instructions on how to complete a verse study.

Ephesians 6:12

1. Verse:

2. Paraphrase:

3. Questions:

4. Cross-references:

5. Personal Application:

Lesson 7

LIVING A GODLY LIFE

Introduction

This week's lesson delves into ways that we can live a godly life. Paul will be pointing out to us that we live in a time when "people will not endure sound teaching, but having itching ears they will accumulate for themselves teachers to suit their own likings, and will turn away from listening to the truth and wander into myths" (2 Timothy 4:3–4).

As I've been thinking about how this happens, I came across a number of quotes that said we are the average of the five people we spend the most time with. Whether or not that is statistically proven, I can't deny that the Bible talks a lot about the impact that friends have on our spiritual lives. We're told in Proverbs 13:20 that "he who walks with wise men becomes wise, but the companion of fools will suffer harm."

What does this have to do with discipleship? First of all, in order to be people who can disciple others well, we need to choose wisely whom *we* follow. In the same way that Paul predicted a time when people would have itching ears and choose teachers to suit their own likings, we can choose to spend time only with people who tell us what we want to hear.

This week, we're going to be invited to spend some time reflecting on whom we follow and end up imitating (consciously or not). We'll then take some time to consider whom we might invite to draw closer to our lives, allowing them to see us as we truly are.

As we endeavor to live with discipleship in mind—aware of whom we are following and who is following us—it's my prayer that we would have humble, teachable hearts. Truth can be spoken from all sorts of different people, and most of us don't really like to be corrected. But a wise woman who is pursuing a godly life will be grateful for anything that gives her insight into how she can run her race well.

Day One
WHOM DO YOU FOLLOW?

Read 2 Timothy 3:10–13.

Throughout this week, we have learned from Paul's writing how to be aware of the darkness of sin that surrounds us and how to guard ourselves against it. Today, we shift direction: Paul has told us what to avoid and now he will tell us where to lean in.

1. A. List out the seven things that Timothy observed in Paul according to 2 Timothy 3:10.

Remember that Paul and Timothy's relationship went much deeper than that of coworkers laboring for the same cause. They were so close that Paul considered Timothy to be a spiritual son. And throughout their time together, Timothy followed him closely in every way. Timothy sought to conform himself to Paul's way of life for the sake of conforming himself to Christ. This is the nature of discipleship—a relationship of love rooted in God, focused on living for Christ, and sharing His gospel.

   B. What did Paul tell the early church in 1 Corinthians 11:1?

An article by FOCUS explains: "Discipleship can be summed up with one biblical key word: imitation. To be a disciple meant you were following a rabbi, a teacher. But the goal of a disciple wasn't merely to master the rabbi's teachings; instead, it was to master his way of life: how he prayed, studied, taught, served the poor and lived out his relationship with God day to day."[27]

---

[27] "'In the Dust of the Rabbi: Living as a Disciple of Jesus,'" FOCUS (24 January, 2022): https://focusequip. org/in-the-dust-of-the-rabbi-living-as-a-disciple-of-jesus/.

Our culture has been infiltrated by influencers—men and women who share their lives on social media so that other people will follow them, buy what they wear, eat what they eat, and do what they do. Each of us will involuntarily choose to follow someone and in doing so will become more like them.

C. With whom do you spend the most time? What are they like? How might you be following them? What accounts do you follow on social media? What is it about them that appeals to you?

D. Consider the traits that Paul listed about himself. He could confidently tell others to follow him because he was certain that he was following Jesus. The goal was not to lead others to himself but to Christ. Think of the women in your life who exhibit the characteristics he mentioned. Do you follow them? If not, how could you spend more time with them and learn?

2. Read 2 Timothy 3:11. In what other circumstances did Timothy follow Paul, and what did Paul say God did for him?

In following Paul, Timothy learned from Paul just how much suffering and persecution must be endured for the gospel, but he also witnessed God's deliverance through it all. Paul showed Timothy how to suffer well, with faith and gratitude. This was a lesson that would serve Timothy well as he carried on the torch of faith after Paul's passing.

3. Think again of the women in your life who exhibit the traits that Paul listed. How do they handle suffering and persecution? How can you see that the Lord has delivered them? How can you learn from them?

Quiet your heart and enjoy His presence…He will see you through even the most difficult circumstances.

Dear Lord,

Just as I've been called to follow others who are ahead of me in life and faith, I'm called to be that model for those who are in my circle of influence. As I think about the sufferings and persecutions I've already faced, I can see ways in which You have delivered me. Help me to have a heart of gratitude that doesn't forget the fact that even when I was in the midst of circumstances that felt unending and so hard to endure, You got me through. I am still here. I am still standing.

May this perspective on my past help me in my present. There are people who are observing me in the midst of my current difficulties and they want to see if Christ makes a difference. Help me to be a steadfast, patient, loving woman in the midst of my sufferings. Amen.

Day Two
A BETTER WAY THAN BAD TO WORSE

Read 2 Timothy 3:12–13.

1. A. What does Paul believe in light of the persecutions he faced according to 2 Timothy 3:12?

   B. Do you agree with Paul? Why or why not? Have you experienced any kind of persecution because of your desire to live a godly life? Take a moment to write about your experience.

2. A. Having contrasted his behavior with the behavior of false teachers, Paul turned his attention again to the behavior of those who refuse to follow God. What did he say in 2 Timothy 3:13?

B. Have you experienced this in your life? What happened, and how did you stop or correct the course?

3. The story is told of a young man who grew up in an incredibly broken home. Just as Paul described, those in his environment refused to follow God, and things went from bad to worse.

A couple from his local church began inviting the young man to dine with them on a regular basis. Unlike his experience of the house in which he grew up, this couple loved Jesus and tried to raise their family according to His plan. The young man eventually told the couple that he had never seen a family that, though still imperfect, worked so well. The husband began to mentor the young man, teaching him to become a good husband and father. Although the young man was raised in a chaotic and destructive environment, all he had to do was experience a family life well lived to know that he wanted what they had.

Many in our society have experienced deep brokenness in their homes, their schools, and their friendships, and have no idea what it looks like to believe in Jesus and follow Him. They have no idea that there is a better way to live. What if our lives looked so much like Jesus that a witness could notice that there was something else—something better—and know that it can be achieved? But what if they began to witness that "better way" in us? Who might you invite into your home to experience the love of Christ and the difference He makes?

Jesus declares that we are to be "the salt of the earth," making food; making life taste better, taste the way it should. We want to live in such a way as to give others a taste that goodness is real and believable. We want to live as a sign that points reliably to Him.

Quiet your heart and enjoy His presence…May He impress on your heart those He wants you to follow.

Dear Lord,

Show me whom You want me to follow so that I can learn on a practical level how to be more like You. So often I know how I should live, but I don't know how to implement it into my daily life. But You have placed women in my life who are a few steps ahead of me and who know how to do this well. There are a few women who come to mind [.] Thank you for their witness and please open the opportunity for me to follow them more closely.

Lord, what person am I following that is leading me away from You? Who in my real life? Who on social media? What celebrities and artists do I want to emulate whose lives and choices are far from You? Give me the eyes to see through their messages and lead me to influencers who are following You.

Finally, Lord, as I follow others, I ask You to make me someone worthy of following. Help me to center every aspect of my life on You, from how I speak to how I spend my money to how I spend my time, structure my family, and treat my friends. Give me the wisdom that I need to show someone else that life with You is the best life there is. I know You call me to do this, Lord. Give me all that I need to fulfill Your call. Amen.

Day Three
FINDING WHOLENESS IN THE SCRIPTURES

Read 2 Timothy 3:14–17.

1.   A. How did Paul instruct Timothy in 2 Timothy 3:14–15?

Remember that Timothy received a deep understanding of the Old Testament scriptures from his devout Jewish mother, Eunice, and grandmother Lois.

B. Deuteronomy 6 gives us an idea of the gravity with which Israelites took knowing and passing on God's law. How did Moses instruct the Israelites in Deuteronomy 6:6–9?

Devout Jews followed these instructions to the letter. Even today, devout Jews bind their arms with God's scriptures during their morning prayers by wearing small black boxes with leather straps that contain God's word. Timothy's mother and grandmother would have given him rigorous training in God's word from the time when he was very young.

Paul's words to Timothy, "but as for you," were the line in the sand. The world might act one way, but Timothy was set apart for a higher purpose—for God's purpose. And living out that difference would be accomplished not only through what he already knew about God from his upbringing but from his new understanding of the Scriptures in light of Jesus.

2. A. Early in this Bible study, we explored what kind of faith you received from your family. Hopefully, some of it was good, and some of it might have led you astray or caused barriers to your relationship with God later in life. Revisiting what you learned about God when you were younger is beneficial. What was it? How might that knowledge of Him call you to live set apart from the world?

B. Now apply Paul's phrase to Timothy to your one life.
The world reveres status, wealth, and celebrity. But as for you _____.
The world encourages selfish living. But as for you _____.
The world preaches that we should do what makes us happy or makes us feel good. But as for you _____.
The world teaches that suffering is a bad thing. But as for you _____.

3. A. How did Paul describe the sacred writings in 2 Timothy 3:16–17?

    B. Other translations of the Bible say that all scripture is "God-breathed." How does the Church explain the truth that the scriptures are inspired by God, or God-breathed? Read *CCC* 101, 105, and 106 and sum up the teaching.

4. Can you think of a time when God spoke directly to your heart while you were reading the Bible? What was the scripture? What did He say? How does this help you to experience God's inspiration when you read the Bible?

Quiet your heart and enjoy His presence…Let His word guide you into His truth.

"Thy word is a lamp unto my feet" (Psalm 119:105).

Dear Lord,

You breathe the words of scripture afresh to me as I read them. Thank You for continuously coming down to me, in Jesus Christ becoming man, in Jesus Christ becoming a piece of bread that can fit into my hand and travel to my heart, and in Your word written and transmitted to me through the ages as an incredible gift to all who choose to read it. Please show me what You think of me in Your word and teach me how to stand firm in that identity. As I read the Bible, please dispel all the lies I've believed so that I can live with a free mind that is conformed to Yours. Please correct my action and lead me to repentance so that I can tell others how I met Your unending mercy when I opened Your word. I ask You to lead me to the practical examples of those who have gone before me, whose lives are chronicled in the Bible—they show me what to do and what not to do when I am trying to follow You. Help me to see that time spent in Your word is never wasted, that You always meet me there. Give me the grace of a strong memory so that I can remember what I read and hold fast to it during the day. Amen.

Day Four
LIVING DISCIPLESHIP

Read 2 Timothy 4:1–2.

1. As Paul nears the end of his letter, his tone becomes even more urgent than it had been before. What did Paul give to Timothy in 2 Timothy 4:1? In whose presence, and how did he describe them?

2. What else did Paul want Timothy to be aware of, according to 2 Timothy 4:1?

What would change in our behavior if we knew that Christ was coming back in two years? It is so hard for us to even wrap our minds around such a thing. What if we had concrete proof that He was coming back in the next six months? Would the churches overflow? Would we worship with a level of sincerity? Would we urgently share the good news, desperate to have our loved ones at our side when Christ returned?

It's hard to believe that we will see Jesus return in our lifetimes, but many people experience His coming every day when they pass from this earth to the next. Knowing that one day each of us will stand before God's throne, let us embrace the urgency that Paul was trying to transmit.

3. A. What did Paul solemnly urge Timothy to do in 2 Timothy 4:2?

    B. Can you think of a time when you shared about your faith in an unfavorable situation? What was the outcome? Can you think of a time when you knew in your heart that you were supposed to speak about Jesus and you didn't?

Even if the conditions are unfavorable, God knows more than we do. He might be calling us to plant a seed that will blossom later, without our knowledge. He may use our words to reach *one person* out of an uninterested crowd. Sometimes He asks us to speak up simply to help us cultivate courage or humility.

    C. What is the difference between being serious about sharing God's word and falling into the idea that it is we who are in charge of saving souls?

God always initiates and always saves, not us. Pope Saint John XXIII would finish a day's work and tell God: "Well, I did my best. It's Your church, so I'm going to bed now."[28]

4. Part of preaching the Word of God involves taking the extra steps that Paul describes in 2 Timothy 4:2: convince, rebuke, and encourage.

Convince

A. Think of a time when someone convinced you of something, even if it was buying Cutco knives or essential oils. What was it about their life or their speech that changed your thinking? How can you take a lesson from that experience when telling others about Christ?

Rebuke

It's worth noting that Paul is talking to Timothy, who was a bishop in the Church. When he was called to rebuke those he was pastoring, we can't make a direct application to ourselves. That being said, we are called to speak the truth in love to one another (Ephesians 4:15). Bishop Robert Baron said, "Love without truth devolves into sentimentality. Truth without love becomes cold and calculated." Romans 2:4 tells us that it is the kindness of God that leads us to repentance.

---

[28] "Pope Saint John XXIII," Open Light Media (26 January, 2023): https://openlightmedia.com/saint/st-john-xxiii/.

B. Think of a time when someone corrected you in love. Have you ever wished that someone would've corrected you sooner? What can you learn from that experience when offering corrections to someone else?

Encourage

C. Who in your life needs your encouragement before your correction?

Quiet your heart and enjoy His presence…Let His Spirit give you the words to say.

Dear Lord,

You call me to speak, but all too often I don't even know what to say. I feel awkward because I am afraid of being rejected. I am keenly aware of how little I know of You and how I do not measure up. I also live in a society that teaches me that it is impolite to tell people about You. Yet You are the best thing that could ever happen to someone. As I look out at a world obsessed with self-help and feel-good mantras, help me to remember that they are actually reaching for You. Help me to remember not that I am not offering a new set of rules for them to learn but a genuine relationship with You, the love for whom they are longing. I might not have the words, but You do. I might not feel prepared, but You dwell in me. I might be so aware of my faults and failures that I feel that I am not the person to speak, but You say I am Yours, and because I belong to You, that is enough to invite someone else in. Lord, give me Your strength, Your wisdom, Your words. Give me Your discernment. Give me Your boldness and Your patience. In the end, it is You who initiates, You who call, and You who save. Amen.

Day Five
ROOTED IN TRUTH

Read 2 Timothy 4:3–5.

"Truth doesn't change according to our ability to stomach it."—Flannery O'Connor

1. Paul continues to warn Timothy against the age, instruct him how to guard himself, and continue the ministry. What does Paul say in 2 Timothy 4:3?

Does this sound familiar? In much of our society, teaching has become synonymous with rationalization. No matter what you believe, you can find a Christian church that preaches a Jesus who wants you to do whatever you already want. Pop culture is filled with celebrities with tons of money and massive platforms who teach something that looks like Christianity but isn't. They espouse Christian principles mixed in with new-age practices. They preach secular morality that places no boundaries on sexuality, substance use, or material consumption. It is easy to find a "religion" or "authority" that approves any desire, no matter how disordered. The problem is that these teachings are not Christianity and they will not bring us peace or happiness.

2. How does *CCC* 405 help us to understand why people are drawn to follow belief systems that are contrary to Christianity?

3. A. In the first half of 2 Timothy 4:4, Paul explained that people who have itching ears only want to listen to teachings that affirm them. Where will they ultimately wander, according to the second half of 2 Timothy 4:4?

A myth is a widely held but false belief or idea. In this instance, Paul was specifically speaking about false beliefs, ideas, and practices having to do with religion, and they lead those who believe in them into practices that go against God's will.

   B. Buying into myths, whether we realize it or not, will inevitably lead to superstition, idolatry, or divinization. What does the *Catechism of the Catholic Church* say about these things?

   • **Superstition.** See *CCC* 2111.

- **Idolatry.** See *CCC* 2113.

- **Divinization.** See *CCC* 2116.

C. For deeper insight into modern forms of superstition, idolatry, and divinization, see Appendix 6. Have you fallen into any of these practices? If so, how? Take a moment to ask God to help you to reject them and bring you back into the Truth.

4. Having again warned Timothy against the ways of the world, what four things does Paul remind him to do to stay rooted in Christ and true to his ministry? See 2 Timothy 4: 5.

Quiet your heart and enjoy His presence…His Spirit will guide you into all Truth.

Dear Lord,

Please reveal to me any way that I have embraced a false teaching just because it makes me feel good. Lord, show me where I have participated in practices that drag me away from You and remind me that it is You, always You, who is on my side.

In the name of the Lord Jesus Christ, I reject Satan. In the name of the Lord Jesus Christ, I reject all his works. In the name of the Lord Jesus Christ, I reject all his empty promises. In the name of the Lord Jesus Christ, I renounce and repent of any way that I have knowingly or unknowingly taken part in Satan's plan. Lord, I accept the Truth that Your way will lead me to everlasting life. Give me the eyes to see the world as You see it. Give me Your heart to love what is good. Give me the eyes to see myself as You see me. Teach me to gravitate toward Your truth and walk away from that lie so that I can stay true to You and the call You have placed on me in this life. Amen.

Conclusion

"Since we are surrounded by so great a cloud of witnesses, let us also lay aside every weight, and sin which clings so closely, and let us run with perseverance the race that is set before us" (Hebrews 12:1).

We are surrounded by witnesses in Heaven who have imitated Christ while on earth and are now cheering for us on the other side of eternity. We have witnesses around us who are ahead of us in spiritual maturity, giving us clear examples to follow. And we have people witnessing our behavior, hopefully being inspired to follow Jesus by us.

When we're encouraged to walk away from superstitions, idolatry, and divinization, it's never to spoil our fun. It's to help us to lay aside the weights that are holding us back from running our race to the finish line.

In our next two lessons, we're going to be focusing on finishing well. No matter what point we are at in life, there can be behaviors, relationships, and disordered desires that are dragging us down. Let's cast them off so we can run with steadfastness and patience, keeping our eye on what matters most.

Want to learn more about this topic? Don't miss this lesson's short video from Mallory at walkingwithpurpose.com/videos.

My Resolution

In what specific way will I apply what I learned in this lesson?

Examples:

1. After reflecting on whose behavior I want to emulate, I'll take a look at the accounts I follow on social media and unfollow any that are drawing me away from, instead of closer to, God.

2. After reading Appendix 6, I'll go to the sacrament of Reconciliation to confess any participation in superstition, idolatry, and divinization.

3. I will take some extended time to pray with Paul's instruction to Timothy from day one: "convince, rebuke, and encourage, with the utmost patience in teaching." I will write down why I am convinced that Jesus is the way, the truth, and the life. What about my belief should be convincing to others? I will explore what it means to me to rebuke with a spirit of joy and love. I will ask the Lord how He wants me to be encouraging to others. I will then simplify what I have written so that I can remember these principles as I can easily implement them into my relationships.

My Resolution:

Catechism Clips

CCC 101 In order to reveal himself to men, in the condescension of his goodness, God speaks to them in human words: "Indeed the words of God, expressed in the words of men, are in every way like human language, just as the Word of the eternal Father, when he took on himself the flesh of human weakness, became like men."

CCC 105 God is the author of Sacred Scripture. "The divinely revealed realities, which are contained and presented in the text of Sacred Scripture, have been written down under the inspiration of the Holy Spirit. For Holy Mother Church, relying on the faith of the apostolic age, accepts as sacred and canonical the books of the Old and the New Testaments, whole and entire, with all their parts, on the grounds that, written under the inspiration of the Holy Spirit, they have God as their author, and have been handed on as such to the Church herself."

CCC 106 God inspired the human authors of the sacred books. "To compose the sacred books, God chose certain men who, all the while he employed them in this task, made full use of their own faculties and powers so that, though he acted in them and by them, it was as true authors that they consigned to writing whatever he wanted written, and no more."

CCC 405 Although it is proper to each individual, original sin does not have the character of a personal fault in any of Adam's descendants. It is a deprivation of original holiness and justice, but human nature has not been totally corrupted: it is wounded in the natural powers proper to it; subject to ignorance, suffering, and the dominion of death; and inclined to sin—an inclination to evil that is called "concupiscence." Baptism, by imparting the life of Christ's grace, erases original sin and turns a man back toward God, but the consequences for nature, weakened and inclined to evil, persist in man and summon him to spiritual battle.

CCC 2111 Superstition is the deviation of religious feeling and of the practices this feeling imposes. It can even affect the worship we offer the true God, e.g., when one attributes an importance in some way magical to certain practices otherwise lawful or necessary. To attribute the efficacy of prayers or of sacramental signs to their mere external performance, apart from the interior dispositions that they demand, is to fall into superstition.

CCC 2113 Idolatry not only refers to false pagan worship. It remains a constant temptation to faith. Idolatry consists in divinizing what is not God. Man commits idolatry whenever he honors and reveres a creature in place of God, whether this be gods or demons (for example, satanism), power, pleasure, race, ancestors, the state, money, etc. Jesus says, "You cannot serve God and mammon." Many martyrs died for not adoring "the Beast," refusing even to simulate such worship. Idolatry rejects the unique Lordship of God; it is therefore incompatible with communion with God.

CCC 2116 All forms of divination are to be rejected: recourse to Satan or demons, conjuring up the dead or other practices falsely supposed to "unveil" the future. Consulting horoscopes, astrology, palm reading, interpretation of omens and lots, the phenomena of clairvoyance, and recourse to mediums all conceal a desire for power over time, history, and, in the last analysis, other human beings, as well as a wish to conciliate hidden powers. They contradict the honor, respect, and loving fear that we owe to God alone.

Verse Study

See Appendix 4 for instructions on how to complete a verse study.

Jude 1:18

1. Verse:

2. Paraphrase:

3. Questions:

4. Cross-references:

5. Personal Application:

 NOTES

Lesson 8

FINISHING WELL

Introduction

On the morning of September 8, 2022, the world stopped to remember the life of a woman who, despite all odds, had lived well and finished her life well. Queen Elizabeth II died at the age of ninety-six, completing a seventy-year reign as queen of England.

In 1947, four years before she became the queen, she turned twenty-one and made a promise to the people of the British Commonwealth:

> I declare before you all that my whole life, whether it be long or short, shall be devoted to your service and the service of our great imperial family to which we all belong. But I shall not have the strength to carry out this resolution alone unless you join in with me, as I now invite you to do: I know that your support will be unfailingly given. God help me to make good my vow, and God bless all of you who are willing to share in it.[29]

Seventy-four years later, the world judged that she had fulfilled that promise; at the news of her passing, millions paused their lives to mourn her death and celebrate her life.

Queen Elizabeth II is a modern example of someone who aimed for a life of service, nobility, and loyalty. Through commitment, perseverance, and faith in God, she arrived at the end of her life having accomplished her goals and had inspired the world.

---

[29] Queen Elizabeth, "A Speech by the Queen on her 21 Birthday, 1947" (21 February, 2023): https://www.royal.uk/21st-birthday-speech-21-april-1947.

In the Catholic Church, we celebrate those who finish well in our tradition of honoring the saints. Thousands of men and women have gone before us. Not every saint began well, but all finished well. They are saints because God's love captivated them and living for Him became their entire pursuit. Who are some of these women?

We behold the everyday life of Saint Zelie Martin, who began her life in love with God, lived simply, and finished even more in love with Him. Her life is an invitation to all mothers to love God first and raise their children to become saints. Zelie and her husband, Louis, had nine children together. Four of them died at an early age. Zelie carried this incredible heartache with grace, trusting in God's will. She worked in a home-based industry as one of France's finest lace makers and raised her family, dealing with many of the same difficulties of mothers today. Zelie suffered from breast cancer for twelve years before she died in 1877. Her love for God until her last moments was not diminished by her suffering (though she writes of the difficulties), but deepened. She and Louis raised five daughters who all entered religious life. Today we know their youngest daughter as Saint Thérèse of Lisieux, Doctor of the Church.

We also celebrate the life of the servant of God Dorothy Day as someone who did not begin well but certainly finished well. Dorothy Day was an American journalist and social activist. She lived a bohemian lifestyle at the beginning of her life: she entered two common-law marriages, suffered an abortion, and eventually birthed her daughter, Tamar, out of wedlock. After the birth of her daughter, she began her journey toward God and the Catholic Church. She was baptized in 1927. Dorothy Day ended her love-with-grit life passionately fighting for the poor and fully committed to the teachings of the Church. No matter our past, we can always turn to God and finish our race running into His arms.

This week we will complete our study of Paul's letter to Timothy, and as we do, I hope you feel the weight of Paul's incredibly well-lived life. Let's see the passion of this disciple as an invitation to love God and make him known with the same level of commitment until the very end.

From the moment Paul met Jesus on the road to Damascus, Paul gave Him everything. Through God's generous grace, He stirred and sustained Paul's flame of faith and held him steady until the end. Paul knew he had reached his goal and wanted Timothy to be able to do the same. Closing his letter, he heightened the urgency, to ensure that

Timothy had all he needed to carry the torch of faith so that he, like Paul, would be equipped to finish well.

Dear sister, as we read these final paragraphs, I pray that you resolve forever to follow the way of discipleship. Do not let the fire that holds you here burn out! Instead, heed Paul's words to Timothy and receive these words as your own. Behold the lives of these two men and the examples above. This kind of living is not just for those who lived in the distant past—it is for us now. What kind of life will you be able to offer to Jesus when your time comes? The well-lived life is one lived completely for God and His kingdom, in which we become saints. This is the life that earns the words "Well done, my good and faithful servant." Let it be us who hears them.

"The only tragedy in life, the only real failure is not to become a saint."—Leon Bloy

Day One
KEEPING THE FAITH

Read 2 Timothy 4:6–7.

With Paul having given final warning and instruction, today we again get a glimpse into Paul and Timothy's close relationship. Timothy's task was to carry the torch of faith, to continue to bring the gospel to new hearts and places, and to shepherd the church well. Paul's task now was to turn to Christ, lay his life down, and finish the race he had started. Imagine sitting in the cell with Paul as he reflected on the life he had led, all he had fought for, and all he had suffered for Christ. This is what it looks like to finish well.

1. A. To what does Paul compare himself? What time is it for him according to 2 Timothy 4:6?

A libation is an ancient sacrificial rite in which a cup of wine or oil is poured out in sacrifice to the gods. The Romans poured out a libation as a gift to the gods at every meal. Jacob and King David are also recorded in the Bible as pouring out drink offerings to God. The imagery here is beautiful. Paul viewed his entire life, including his coming execution, as a gift to God poured out to the last drop.

B. In 1 Corinthians 9, Paul gave us insight into how he was trying to live. To what did he compare a life lived for Christ? How did he say Christians are supposed to compete in 1 Corinthians 9:24–25?

2. As Paul reached the end of his race, how did he evaluate himself according to 2 Timothy 4:7?

3. A. What specifically should our lives look like if we want to finish and proclaim that we have fought the good fight and finished the race? Where should our unwavering loyalty lie, according to Hebrews 10:36–37?

B. What characteristics should we emulate if we are to fight well, according to Galatians 5:22–23?

C. It is the presence of the Holy Spirit in our lives that gives us the grace to stay close to God and live the fruits of the Spirit. What else are we called to do in the power of the Holy Spirit to fight the good fight well? See Acts 1:8.

If we are going to get to the end of our lives having emulated Paul, we must choose to be disciples who stay close to God, exhibit the fruits of His Spirit, and witness to others.

4. A. Is there someone you know who got to the end of their life having fought the good fight for the faith? Who was it? What were they like? Why would you say that they finished well?

B. Imagine what it would look like for you to finish the race and fight the good fight. Take a moment and write about it.

Quiet your heart and enjoy His presence...ask the Lord to help you to persevere.

The story is told of the last marathoner finally entering an Olympic stadium, hours behind the runner in front of him. Most of the spectators had already left. Nevertheless, this Tanzanian athlete limped in, grimacing with every step he took, bleeding and bandaged. He pressed on with his focus on the finish line even though he had no speed, no hope of winning a medal, or any of the accolades the earlier runners had received. When asked why he stayed in the race and didn't give up, he replied, "My country did not send me five thousand miles away to start the race. They sent me five thousand miles away to finish it."[30]

Dear Lord,

I don't know which men won the medals that day at the Olympics, but I remember this story of John Stephen Akhwari. His example encourages me to press on, even if I am limping. But I ask You, please "strengthen [my] weak hands, and make firm [my] feeble knees" (Isaiah 35:3). May I hear Your voice saying, you "who are of a fearful heart, be strong, fear not!" (Isaiah 35:4). Amen.

Day Two
THE CROWN OF RIGHTEOUSNESS

Read 2 Timothy 4:8.

1. Having declared that he ran the race well, what did Paul say was reserved for Him in 2 Timothy 4:8? Who else will receive this?

---

[30] (18 October, 1968):https://olympics.com/en/news/marathon-man-akhwari-demonstrates-superhuman-spirit.

2.   What did Jesus promise in Revelation 2:10?

The crown of life of which Jesus and Paul speak is life in Heaven, the ultimate reward after a life filled with hardship and suffering for the sake of Christ. What a gift for him to know that his heavenly reward awaited.

Most of us believe or understand the concept of Heaven, but we have no idea what Heaven will be like. And if we are honest with ourselves, popular portrayals of Heaven make it seem a bit boring. What do we do up there with the little cherubim? What will it be like to live in perfection? Yet 1 Corinthians 2:9 reminds us that we can't even fathom what Heaven will actually be like: "What no eye has seen, nor ear heard, nor the human heart conceived, what God has prepared for those who love him." We might not be able to understand what Heaven will be like, but one thing is certain: it will not be boring. It will be absolutely glorious—fulfillment, love, and joy beyond our wildest imaginings.

3.   What insight does the Church give us about Heaven in *CCC* 1024 and *CCC* 1025?

1 Corinthians 13:12 reminds us, "For now we see in a mirror, dimly, but then we will see face to face. Now I know only in part; then I will know fully, even as I have been fully known."

Do you ever stop to think about the moment that the veil will be finally pulled away? Do you ever consider that one day you will receive the Eucharist, the body, blood, soul, and divinity of Christ, hidden in the form of bread, for the last time before you will see Him face to face? Do you ever sit in awe at the realization that this world is the world of shadows, but in Heaven there are none—that the world to come is far more real than the one in which we live? Heaven is the goal, the prize given to all who hold firm and "long for his appearing" (2 Timothy 4:8). Let us prepare ourselves so that when our time comes, we, like Paul, can confidently accept the crown of righteousness inscribed with our name.

4. Take a moment and ponder the glorious reality of Heaven. How have you typically thought about Heaven? Does the church's description change the way you think about Heaven? If so, how? How might living for the goal of Heaven help you to live well on earth?

Quiet your heart and enjoy His presence…He is the ultimate fulfillment of all you desire.

Dear Lord,

"For life is to be with Christ; where Christ is, there is life, there is the kingdom."—Saint Ambrose

I confess that I don't always long for Heaven like I should. In all honesty, when I think about it, I think about some sort of illustrated version of Heaven. I think about a place with lots of clouds and angels floating around. I think of a place painted in pastels and wonder what it will be like when I am no longer on this earth. You tell me that Heaven is different from that. Although I may not be able to picture it, a place where I can see You face to face is the place where I ultimately want to be. The idea of me beholding You beyond the veil of this earth seems like it will never come, yet one day it will be here. Gift me with a heart that is grateful for the present moment but also longs for the moment when I am finally in Your complete and eternal presence. Give me a heart that loves Your creation for how it reflects You but longs for the day that there need be no more reflecting because You will be in front of me. Knowing that this day will one day be here, please give me the gift of wisdom to live each moment as though it matters in the next, to order my priorities according to Your desires, so that at the end of my race, I will have finished well. Amen.

Day Three
CONNECTED TO THE CHURCH

Read 2 Timothy 4:9–15.

1. A. What request did Paul make of Timothy in 2 Timothy 4:9?

B. After he asked Timothy to come quickly, Paul revealed his sadness. Those who were close to him at one point had abandoned him or were out on other journeys. Who was no longer with Paul and why, according to 2 Timothy 4:10?

Professor George Montague insightfully compares Paul's feeling to Jesus's in the garden of Gethsemane. "Paul feels the same human need as Jesus felt in the garden when he told his three intimate disciples, 'My soul is sorrowful even until death. Remain here and keep watch with me'" (Matthew 26:38).

Just as Jesus felt alone and abandoned before his death, Paul experienced the pain of abandonment and loneliness. For years he was one of the main leaders in the early Church. He had friends and connections all over the known world as they worked to build the Church. But as time went on and Paul's time in prison lengthened, some relationships failed, and people became busy. Now, in his last hours, that feeling of loneliness moved Paul to beckon his dearest friend to his side.

C. Have you experienced a time when you longed for the comfort of a companion who really understands? Were you able to find such a friend? Did it make a difference?

2. A. Who was with Paul? Who else did Paul tell Timothy to bring and why according to 2 Timothy 4:11?

This is the same Luke who wrote the Gospel of Luke. He had ventured out on this missionary journey with Paul and ended up in jail with him. Just imagine, these giants of the faith suffering together in prison.

Mark is John Mark, who authored the Gospel of Mark, and Paul's request to see him gives us remarkable insight into the relationships forged in the early Church. Here we find a story that reveals the brokenness of the church and the power of God's reconciliation.

B. Read Acts 15:36–41. What happened between Paul and his companion Barnabas concerning John Mark?

CCC 817 reminds us, "Where there are sins, there are also divisions, schisms, heresies, and disputes. Where there is virtue, however, there also is harmony and unity, from which arise the one heart and one soul of all believers." In this instance we see the very human sins and irritations of apostles and the unity that arises out of virtue.

It is evident that Paul and John Mark have reconciled and are again unified in their mission—so much so that Paul asked for his presence at the end of his life.

C. Consider your experience in the Church. Where do you see its beauty? Have you experienced its dysfunction? Have you ever had an experience of reconciliation similar to Paul's? What was the situation? How did reconciliation come about and what were its effects?

3. What did Paul ask Timothy to bring to him in 2 Timothy 13?

What was it that Paul needed in his last hours? He needed a friend, some warmth, and above all, the scriptures. Even in his last moments, it was the members of his Church and the Word of God that brought him the most comfort.

4. Paul mentions abandonment and loneliness, but in 2 Timothy 4:14–15, he mentions betrayal. Who betrayed him? What is his response and what does he warn Timothy about?

Quiet Your heart and enjoy his presence…He takes what is broken and makes it beautiful.

Dear Lord,

You know better than anyone else the messiness of Your Church. Honestly, it can sometimes feel hard to defend it to a world that looks at our Church and only sees hypocrisy. It can be hard to explain it to others who think its rules are unloving and its message completely out of touch. Even walking in the door, I can easily see that there is much brokenness. I experience it and I perpetuate it. Yet You who were abandoned in Your moment of need asked those same men to carry on Your message! You continue to offer Yourself to every generation through this Church. Despite the brokenness, despite appearances, You have offered us Your presence in Your Church. It is a refuge, a rock, and a firm foundation for all who are willing to hold its treasure. Help me to see it for what it is—a gift. Help me to speak about it to others as a gift, an imperfect vessel through which You make saints. Amazing. Lord, I repent of the ways that I have refused to stay connected to my local church, whether it be out of pride or genuine hurt, and I ask You to open a door for me. Please lay out a path so that I can stay connected to other women who are striving to love like You. Please bring about reconciliation in my heart. I ask You to pour out a spirit of unity in my local church so that when people walk in, they no longer see the brokenness of its people but the joy and redemption You offer. Amen.

Day Four
TOTAL RELIANCE ON GOD

Read 2 Timothy 4:16–18.

1. Paul continued to reveal his anguish to Timothy. What event did he describe in 2 Timothy 4:16? What happened at that event? What was Paul's response?

When Paul spoke about his first defense, he was referring to the process of his trial. Under the Roman system, a trial began with an accusation. In Paul's case, anyone could have brought a complaint to the government against him simply for claiming that Jesus Christ is Lord. That was considered a crime against Rome since Paul was undermining worship of the Roman gods. Once that accusation was accepted, Paul would have been summoned to an interrogation at which the judge would dismiss the case or sign an inscription requiring Paul to attend a first hearing, a trial, a sentencing, and then execution. For fear of suffering the same fate, all of Paul's friends, his colaborers in the vineyard, had abandoned him at his most vulnerable time.

2. Read 2 Timothy 4:17–18. Where did he find his hope? Who stood by him? Sum up what Paul said.

3. A. Read Psalm 22:19–21 and write down the similarities to what Paul said in 2 Timothy 4:17–18.

Theologians believe that Paul was thinking of the words of Psalm 22 when he wrote this.[31] Not only does his writing follow the pattern of the psalm in certain parts, but the psalm begins with the words "My God, my God why have you forsaken me." These are the words that Jesus spoke as he hung on a cross, abandoned by his friends. Paul, experiencing a similar feeling of abandonment, drew comfort from this psalm and the words of his Savior.

Although Paul feels alone in his abandonment, it is not possible for him to actually be alone because Jesus has already entered fully into the experience of being abandoned. Therefore, He was with Paul in his loneliest moments. In fact, it is this same intimacy Paul has with Christ that comforts him, especially to be comforted by the words of his savior in Psalm 22.

B. Consider a time when you were hurting, physically or emotionally. Did someone—a beloved person—enter into it with you? How did that presence amidst your pain change your experience of it? How does feeling entirely alone increase the intensity of emotional or physical pain?

---

[31] Barclay, 248.

C. Can you think of something that you went through in which you felt completely alone? Did you look for *God* in those moments? Why or why not? Did you find Him? If so, how? In what way might He have delivered you from the "lion's mouth" even if you didn't recognize it at the time?

4. In those last moments, Paul stayed true to all he had taught throughout his ministry, proving that he believed what he wrote, even until death. What did Paul preach in Romans 8:35–36? How did Paul live this out in his final moments?

What a beautiful witness to Timothy and to us! Paul walked toward his execution knowing that he could not be separated from Christ, but rather that his execution would drive him right into the arms of Christ. Paul is living proof that we can stay close to Jesus throughout every circumstance. He gives us the power to endure suffering and one day join Him in joy.

5. It is easy to speak the words of scripture that sound right and beautiful, but it is much harder to live them. In reality, the only thing that can separate us from the love of Christ is sin, and even then, God offers us His abundant mercy. But it doesn't always feel that way. It feels like there are a million things that can easily separate us from Christ, whether it be a family tragedy, the loss of a loved one, a circumstance that didn't go the way it was supposed to, a hard relationship with a child, or a million other small things that get in the way. Is there something right now that seems like it is separating you from the love of Christ? What is it? Think of Paul's example. Nothing—not persecution, hunger, abandonment, or even a criminal's execution—could separate him from the love of God. How can this story give you the courage and strength to persevere?

Quiet your heart and enjoy His presence…He will deliver you.

"The Lord will rescue me from every evil and save me for his heavenly kingdom" (2 Timothy 4:18).

Dear Lord,

Reading these words from Paul from prison is very thought-provoking. Just as he is writing that he'll be rescued from every evil, he is writing with chains on his wrists. I'm sitting with this image and am reminded, You don't always rescue us from what we fear, but often rescue us through it. When we call out to You in distress, You always answer. Your answer isn't always to take away what is causing us pain. Your answer always is Your presence. It's the gift of YOU.

There are times when I have questioned whether that really is much help. But if I am honest, the times Your presence has not felt like a game changer to me are the times when I ignore the fact that You are there. I focus on my troubles instead of inviting You into my pain. All too often I turn away instead of leaning in.

Help me in this regard. Woo me to Your heart. Your presence is the true gift, the one thing that changes everything. I believe this, Lord. But help me when I forget. Amen.

Day Five
THE IMPORTANCE OF COMMUNITY

Read 2 Timothy 4:19–22.

Today we come to the end of Paul's letter to Timothy. As Bible teacher Beth Moore said so beautifully: "The ink from the greatest human writer of the New Testament canon went dry." As he came to the end of the words he would write while on earth, it all came back to Jesus and His Church.

1. Read 2 Timothy 4:19–22. Write out the names of the people Paul mentioned in his final greeting as well as Paul's final words in verse 22.

Who were these people Paul mentioned in his last sentences? Prisca and Aquila were a married couple of Jewish heritage who ran a church out of their home. They were exiled from Rome, which led them to spend time building the church in Corinth and Ephesus. It is widely believed that at one point, they risked their lives to save Paul's. They also followed Paul's fate and died as martyrs.

Paul had already mentioned Onesiphorus and his family earlier in his letter. Tradition teaches that Onesiphorus was one of the seventy disciples that Jesus sent out to preach the gospel. He was a bishop in the early church and also died a martyr.

Erastus had worked with Paul to spread the gospel in Macedonia, and Trophimus was a gentile whom Paul had brought into a Jewish temple, the event that caused his first imprisonment.

Eubulus, Pudens, Linus, and Claudia were members of the church in Rome. Scholars believed that Pudens and Claudia were married. It is even possible that Claudia was a British princess who had been sent to Rome, married Pudens, heard about Jesus, and came to believe in the gospel.

Although it was a simple and standard way to close his letters, Paul gave us a great gift with the mention of all these names. From the very beginning, the gospel message has penetrated the hearts of people from every race, color, and creed. From the very beginning, it was ordained that the message of Jesus Christ would go to the ends of the earth. So even though Paul felt desperately alone in his last moments, he was actually part of a network of men and women who had labored with him, loved the Lord, and would eventually follow in his footsteps and die for the faith.

2. Think about the structure of your local church community. What is it like? Are there people in your community who are united in living for Christ and sharing the gospel? Who are they? How do they do this? Are you connected to them? If so, how? If not, write down one thing you can do to get connected.

3. Let's reflect on the whole of our journey through 2 Timothy.

    A. Where have you been encouraged?

B. Where have you been challenged?

C. How are you different closing this book than when you opened it?

4. As you look over the book of 2 Timothy, note specific Bible verses that speak to you in the following ways:

A. Led you into repentance.

B. Trained you in righteous living.

C. Made you more into who God created you to be.

Quiet your heart and enjoy His presence…He will sustain you.

Dear Lord,

Thank you for what You have done in my heart over the past weeks. Thank you especially for teaching me or showing me [ ]. I could study You my entire life and never get close to reaching the end of such knowledge. Thank you for the way you have revealed Yourself to me. Help me to own these truths, to remember them, and to implement them into my life so that every time I meet You in prayer, You transform me, little by little, into Your beautiful image. You have given me the gift of understanding Your servants Paul and Timothy through new eyes. You have given me a new understanding of what it means to know You and make You known. You have given me new insights into Your truths and how to guard myself against competing messages. Thank You, Jesus. Help me to walk forward in my life knowing that I belong to You and that life lived close to You is the only life that can bring true freedom and true joy. It is only by living for You that I can leave the legacy I was meant to leave and share Your message, the message I was made to share. Thank you, Lord Jesus. Bind my heart to Yours and keep me in the shadow of Your wings. Amen.

Conclusion

We just read Paul's last written words, but the story was not quite over yet. After Paul finished his letter, he continued to await his execution in Mamertine Prison in Rome. Ultimately, Roman officials led him to the Aquae Salviae and beheaded him, the type of execution given to Roman citizens.

His friends eventually took his body, buried it in the family tomb of a Roman woman named Matrona, and marked the grave. In the fourth century, Emperor Constantine built a church in memorial to Paul's martyrdom. That church was eventually expanded and became the Basilica of Saint Paul Outside the Walls. Today anyone can visit it and behold the tombstone that reads Paulo Apostolo Mart.

Timothy heeded all that Paul had said. He stayed true to the gospel of Jesus Christ and continued the work of Paul and those who had gone before him. In 97 AD, when he was eighty years old, he tried to stop a procession honoring the Roman goddess Diana. Angry worshippers beat him in the street and stoned him to death.

Years ago, I visited Paul's prison in Rome. I stood in that small room and considered the last days of the apostle. As I did, I began to feel incredibly small, as if I were standing in front of the Grand Canyon. Who was I in the midst of this sea of saints?

The faith that we have received is a faith given through unwavering commitment, suffering, and eventual death. For thousands of years, men and women like Paul and Timothy have received the torch of faith. They followed Paul's call to rekindle the faith they had received. They lived their lives with the goal of passing the faith on to faithful witnesses who could teach also. They boldly and faithfully lived out Jesus' call to make disciples of all nations, and it is due to the multitude of unnamed faithful Christians that each of us has received the endless and unsearchable beauty that is the Catholic faith. We stand on their shoulders. I pray that future generations will stand on ours.

Dear sister, I hope that this Bible study was all that you had hoped and more. I pray that you love Jesus and His Church in deeper ways than when you started. I pray that you learned something new that gave you a better understanding of the role that God has called you to play in His dramatic story. I also pray that you are better equipped than ever to burn brightly with the light of faith and to kindle the light and glory of the Gospel to those who have not yet heard it.

Grace be with you.

Want to learn more about this topic? Don't miss this lesson's short video from Mallory at walkingwithpurpose.com/videos.

My Resolution

In what specific way will I apply what I learned in this lesson?

Examples:

1. I will choose a saint who lived her life well until the finish line and take time to be inspired by her life. The time I normally spend being entertained by a screen, I'll replace with time reading her story.

2. Paul drew comfort from Psalm 22. I will take some time to choose a psalm or verses from a psalm. I will write it down and say it out loud in the moments when I feel alone so that I can remember that God is always with me.

3. I will consider my involvement in my church community. I will think of a woman who has had a major impact on my faith and find a way to thank her. I will then ask the Lord to reveal how He wants me to invest in the next generation. In obedience, I will then take the first step to make it happen.

My Resolution:

Catechism Clips

CCC 1024 This perfect life with the Most Holy Trinity—this communion of life and love with the Trinity, with the Virgin Mary, the angels, and all the blessed—is called "heaven." Heaven is the ultimate end and fulfillment of the deepest human longings and is the state of supreme, definitive happiness.

CCC 1025 To live in heaven is "to be with Christ." The elect live "in Christ," but they retain, or rather find, their true identity, their own name. "For life is to be with Christ; where Christ is, there is life, there is the kingdom."

Verse Study

See Appendix 4 for instructions on how to complete a verse study.

1 Corinthians 9:25

1. Verse:

2. Paraphrase:

3. Questions:

4. Cross-references:

5. Personal Application:

 NOTES

Lesson 9: Connect Coffee Talk

FIGHTING THE GOOD FIGHT

You can view this talk via the accompanying DVD or digital download purchase, or access it online at walkingwithpurpose.com/videos.

"I have fought the good fight, I have finished the race, I have kept the faith. From now on there is laid up for me the crown of righteousness, which the Lord, the righteous judge, will award to me on that day, and not only to me but also to all who have loved his appearing" (2 Timothy 4:7–8).

I. Review of Our Journey through 2 Timothy

II. Running the Marathon

III. Two Tips for the Journey

    A. You Always Have to Take a Leap of Faith

    B. Measure Success by How You Love

Questions for Discussion

1. As you think of Saint Paul's challenge to run your race and keep the faith, how are you feeling? Energized? Weary? What challenges are making persevering difficult for you right now?

2. Share about a time in your life or in the life of someone you know when a leap of faith was required. What was the result?

3. Whom do you want to lower through the roof to Jesus?

Appendices

NOTES

Appendix 1
Saint Thérèse of Lisieux

Patron Saint of Walking with Purpose

Saint Thérèse of Lisieux was gifted with the ability to take the riches of our Catholic faith and explain them in a way that a child could imitate. The wisdom she gleaned from Scripture ignited a love in her heart for her Lord that was personal and transforming. The simplicity of the faith that she laid out in her writings is so completely Catholic that Pope Pius XII said, "She rediscovered the Gospel itself, the very heart of the Gospel."

Walking with Purpose is intended to be a means by which women can honestly share their spiritual struggles and embark on a journey that is refreshing to the soul. It was never intended to facilitate the deepest of intellectual study of Scripture. Instead, the focus has been to help women know Christ: to know His heart, to know His tenderness, to know His mercy, and to know His love. Our logo is a little flower, and that has meaning. When a woman begins to open her heart to God, it's like the opening of a little flower. It can easily be bruised or crushed, and it must be treated with the greatest of care. Our desire is to speak to women's hearts no matter where they are in life, baggage and all, and gently introduce truths that can change their lives.

Saint Thérèse of Lisieux, the little flower, called her doctrine "the little way of spiritual childhood," and it is based on complete and unshakable confidence in God's love for us. She was not introducing new truths. She spent countless hours reading Scripture and she shared what she found, emphasizing the importance of truths that had already been divinely revealed. We can learn so much from her:

> The good God would not inspire unattainable desires; I can, then, in spite of my littleness, aspire to sanctity. For me to become greater is impossible; I must put up with myself just as I am with all my imperfections. But I wish to find the way to go to heaven by a very straight, short, completely new little way. We are in a century of inventions: now one does not even have to take the trouble to

climb the steps of a stairway; in the homes of the rich, an elevator replaces them nicely. I, too, would like to find an elevator to lift me up to Jesus, for I am too little to climb the rough stairway of perfection. So I have looked in the books of the saints for a sign of the elevator I long for, and I have read these words proceeding from the mouth of eternal Wisdom: "He that is a little one, let him turn to me" (Proverbs 9:16). So I came, knowing that I had found what I was seeking, and wanting to know, O my God, what You would do with the little one who would answer Your call, and this is what I found:

"As one whom the mother caresses, so will I comfort you. You shall be carried at the breasts and upon the knees they shall caress you" (Isaiah 66:12–13). Never have more tender words come to make my soul rejoice. The elevator which must raise me to the heavens is Your arms, O Jesus! For that I do not need to grow; on the contrary, I must necessarily remain small, become smaller and smaller. O my God, You have surpassed what I expected, and I want to sing Your mercies. (Saint Thérèse of the Infant Jesus, *Histoire d'une Ame: Manuscrits Autobiographiques* [Paris: Éditions du Seuil, 1998], 244.)

Appendix 2

Conversation Cards

Questions

❇	❇
How would you answer the question, *"Who am I?"*	Fast forward five years. What qualities would you want to be true of you?
❇	❇
Why do you think you are here?	What do you think is the best way to find real love?
❇	❇
What does it mean to you to be happy and live a good life?	What do you think are some good ways to focus on what matters and live up to your truest potential?

Questions

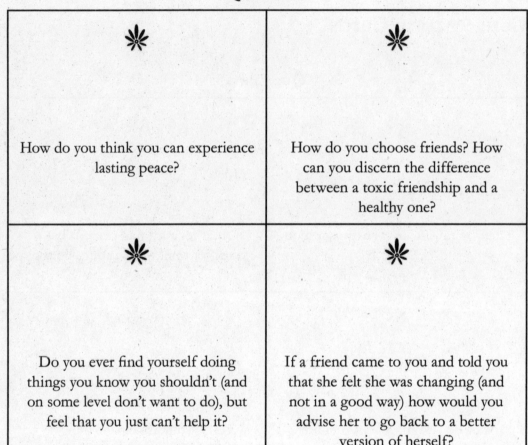

How do you think you can experience lasting peace?

How do you choose friends? How can you discern the difference between a toxic friendship and a healthy one?

Do you ever find yourself doing things you know you shouldn't (and on some level don't want to do), but feel that you just can't help it?

If a friend came to you and told you that she felt she was changing (and not in a good way) how would you advise her to go back to a better version of herself?

Appendix 3

HOW DOES THE HOLY SPIRIT HELP YOU TO OVERCOME FEAR?

Where Fear Comes From

The emotion of fear is neither good nor bad. We can think of it as a kind of alertness, a warning message, a natural response to anything that we perceive will harm us. Its purpose is to keep us safe and prompt us to avoid anything that may truly cause us harm.

Fear is useful when it is properly ordered. The problem is that, due to original sin, the world is disordered and we make disordered choices. *CCC* 405 explains that because of man's fall from grace, human nature "is wounded in the natural powers proper to it, [and human nature is thus] subject to ignorance, suffering and the dominion of death." Because of our human nature, we have to contend with disorder in our faculties. This means it is easy to experience fear in such a way that it prompts us to avoid the wrong danger, the wrong harms, or allow it to exercise mastery over our emotions and passions.

Fear of the future leaves us unable to make decisions in the present, even if there is a very low chance that whatever we fear will ever materialize. Fear of losing a relationship may induce us to be overly possessive of that person and bring dysfunction into the relationship. Fear of being poor might lead us to make unethical choices that harm us and others.

This can easily lead us to experience domination from a spirit of fear. Where fear was meant to serve us and drive us to act responsibly and wisely, it now takes over. It directs all of our decisions and keeps us from joy and freedom.

It's possible that you might be prone to fear and never learned how to deal with it. Slowly but surely, everything inspires fear in your heart and it leaves you paralyzed. It's possible that you experienced a negative event or trauma that, through no fault of your own, has led you to live in fear so that you can avoid a similar situation in the future.

No matter your situation, or how you deal with fear, please know that in a broken world, fear is a formidable force. If this is a struggle for you, you are not alone. Whether you have chosen to embrace fear as a defense mechanism, or it has overcome you without your consent, Jesus has given us His Holy Spirit. He can give you freedom from fear.

Breaking the Cycle of Fear

The Catholic Church teaches that you are a unity of body and a soul. Your body and soul are not compartmentalized—you are a unity. The state of your physical being will affect your spiritual being and what is going on in your heart and soul will reverberate in your body and its physiology.

The more that we allow ourselves to think a certain way, the more we create thought loops in our brain, which causes us to fixate on our fears and anxieties. We also create habits of behavior that train us to serve our fears without even trying.

Part of breaking the cycle of fear requires us to participate in God's plan to break those thought loops and habits. This is rarely accomplished overnight and may require counseling and spiritual direction.

2 Corinthians 10:5 commands us to "Take every thought captive to Christ."

This means that we take stock of our thought-life and then ask, *"Is this true?" "Does this thought match up with God's truth and His word?"* If it does, we let it in. If it doesn't, we renounce it as a lie and replace it **out loud** with God's truth. When we do this, we disrupt our thought-loops and reroute them.

It's important to note that if this were an easy process, our mental health statistics would look far different than they do today. Breaking the cycle of fear can be a difficult process that takes time, and at moments, it may feel like freedom is not possible. Take heart, one more degree of freedom **is** possible. The Lord may be calling you to seek professional help through counseling or spiritual direction. If this is you, do not be afraid to take the next step. Make the phone call or set up the appointment so that someone can walk with you on this journey.

Getting help and taking these steps empowers us to break the power of the spirit of fear.

Note: If you want to begin replacing your thought loops with God's truth, you can visit https://walkingwithpurpose.com/free-printables/ and download the "I Declares," written by Lisa Brenninkmeyer. These are truths from Scripture that you can say out loud to inhabit a new freedom from God, living in his peaceful way of being and renouncing the lies in your thought-life.

The Holy Spirit's Role

In John 16:13 Jesus told us, "When the Spirit of truth comes, he will guide you into all the truth."

We have already learned that because of original sin, it is difficult for us to live ordered lives according to God's will. To accomplish God's will, to live our lives in Christ, the Holy Spirit enables us to rise above our human nature and embody certain virtues that are supernatural, which means they exceed human nature.

When we open ourselves up to the power of the Holy Spirit, He instills in us the supernatural virtue of hope. Hope enables us to look beyond our present circumstances and focus on God's promise that He will always be faithful. Hope leads to courage. With our eyes focused on God, we become capable of facing our fears, or even overcoming them, because we believe that no matter what happens, God will be faithful. The more we allow the Holy Spirit to instill in us the virtue of hope, the less power fear will wield over our lives. According to *CCC* 1817, "Hope is the theological virtue by which we desire the kingdom of heaven and eternal life as our happiness, placing our trust in Christ's promises and relying not on our own strength, but on the help of the grace of the Holy Spirit."

CCC 1818 continues: "The virtue of hope responds to the aspiration to happiness which God has placed in the heart of every man; it takes up the hopes that inspire men's activities and purifies them so as to order them to the Kingdom of heaven; it keeps man from discouragement; it sustains him during times of abandonment;

it opens up his heart in expectation of eternal beatitude. Buoyed up by hope, he is preserved from selfishness and led to the happiness that flows from charity."

Additionally, the Holy Spirit offers us His gifts. These gifts include wisdom, understanding, counsel, fortitude, knowledge, piety, and fear of the Lord. Both fortitude and fear of the Lord enables us to overcome our fears. Fortitude gives us the courage to face our fears because our hope is ultimately in God's faithfulness. And fear of the Lord keeps our minds on His power and His glory. With our sights set on Him, it becomes harder for fear to control us.

If you are struggling with a spirit of fear, I invite you to call upon the Holy Spirit. Tell Him what you are fearing and ask Him to show you why you have that fear. Ask Him to show you the truth and reveal what steps He is leading you to take. Believe that He can lead you into freedom and know that your story is not over. The God of hope uses everything, even your old fears, even your past or present sufferings, to make you holy, but He longs for you to take the steps needed to enable you to put your trust completely in Him and embrace His power, love, and self-control.

"May the God of hope fill you with all joy and peace in believing, so that by the power of the Holy Spirit you may abound in hope." Romans 15:13

Appendix 4
HOW TO DO A VERSE STUDY

A verse study is an exciting Bible study tool that can help to bring the Scriptures to life! By reading, reflecting on, and committing a verse to memory, we open ourselves to the Holy Spirit, who reveals very personal applications of our Lord's words and actions to our daily lives.

Learning to do a verse study is not difficult but it can be demanding. In this Walking with Purpose™ study, a Bible verse has been selected to reinforce a theme of each lesson. To do the verse study, read the verse and then follow these simple instructions. You'll be on your way to a deeper and more personal understanding of Scripture.

- **Read the verse and the paragraph before and after the verse.**

- **Write out the selected verse.**

- **Paraphrase.**

  Write the verse using your own words. What does the verse say?

- **Ask questions.**

  Write down any questions you have about the verse. What does it say that you don't understand?

- **Use cross-references.**

  Look up other Bible verses that help to shed light on what the selected verse means. A study Bible will often list cross-references in the margin or in the study notes. Another excellent resource is Biblos.com. This website allows you to enter a specific Bible verse and it will provide many cross-references and additional insights into the passage of Scripture you selected. Record any insights you gain from the additional verses you are able to find.

- **Make a personal application.**

What does the verse say to you personally? Is there a promise to claim? a warning to heed? an example to follow? Ask God to help you find something from the verse that you can apply to your life.

The recommended Bible translations for use in Walking with Purpose™ studies are: The New American Bible, which is the translation used in the United States for the readings at Mass; The Revised Standard Version, Catholic Edition; and The Jerusalem Bible.

A Sample Verse Study

1. **Verse:**

"I am the vine, you are the branches. Those who abide in me and I in them bear much fruit, because apart from me you can do nothing." (John 15:5)

2. **Paraphrase:**

Jesus is the vine, I am the branch. If I abide in Him, then I'll be fruitful, but if I try to do everything on my own, I'll fail at what matters most. I need Him.

3. **Questions:**

What does it mean to abide? How does Jesus abide in me? What kind of fruit is Jesus talking about?

4. **Cross-references:**

"He that eats my flesh, and drinks my blood, abides in me, and I in him." (John 6:56). This verse brings to mind the Eucharist, and the importance of receiving Christ in the Eucharist as often as possible. This is a very important way to abide in Jesus.

"If you abide in me, and my words abide in you, ask for whatever you wish, and it will be done for you." (John 15:7). How can Jesus' words abide in me if I never read them? I need to read the Bible if I want to abide in Christ.

"It was not you who chose me, but I who chose you and appointed you to go and bear fruit that will remain, so that whatever you ask the Father in my name he may give you." (John 15:16). Not all fruit remains. Some fruit is only good temporarily—on earth. I want my fruit to remain in eternity—to count in the long run.

"The fruit of the Spirit is love, joy, peace, patience, kindness, generosity, faithfulness, gentleness, self-control." (Galatians 5:22–23). These are some of the fruits that will be seen if I abide in Christ.

5. **Personal Application:**

I will study my calendar this week, making note of where I spend my time. Is most of my time spent on things that will last for eternity (fruit that remains)? I'll reassess my priorities in light of what I find.

Appendix 5
MAKING DISCIPLES

Do you recall the introduction from Lesson 3 and the ripple effect of the woman who shared Jesus with me and my friends at her kitchen table? She was farther along in her faith journey than we were, but she did not hold us at arms' length. The relationships she built with us were deep friendships marked by authenticity, love, and true enjoyment of the time we spent together. She was not teaching us about Jesus just to check a box and claim that she had evangelized some people. She showed us Christ in unspoken ways, and also by speaking and teaching us explicitly about the Gospel message. She invited us to go deeper into a relationship with Jesus Christ, challenged us when we went off-course, built us up, and then sent us out.

Maybe you are wondering, *"How can I do this? How can I make disciples in my own life?"* Here is a simple, practical breakdown of steps you can follow as you seek to live as a disciple and make disciples. Please note that although the journey of discipleship is broken apart and explained, it is done so for the sake of simplifying and teaching. The language and directions are meant to help you better understand the process, but discipleship is a journey that only ends when we get to Heaven. Each phase is not meant to completely end but to be revisited again and again—because to live for Christ requires continual conversion. Take these directions and apply them to the specific circumstances of your life so that they serve and encourage you.

The Practicals

True friendship is the foundation for discipleship. In 2 Thessalonians, Paul said to his disciples, "So, being affectionately desirous of you, we were ready to share with you not only the gospel of God but also our own selves, because you had become very dear to us." Discipleship starts with friendship, but the friendship must not be an end in itself. It must be intentionally directed toward Jesus Christ.

The Church recognizes discipleship as a three-phase journey that is commonly called: **Win, Build, Send**. Being familiar with each stage will help you to recognize where you are in your faith journey and guide you as you share your faith with others. Let's take a look at each stage.

Win

The beginning of the disciples journey begins with believing that Jesus is Lord, accepting the Gospel, turning away from sin, and making the decision to live for Christ.

For You: A life of passionate discipleship requires that you continually come back to the basics. These four decisions are not a one-time thing, but a continual profession that Christ is Lord. Preach the Gospel to yourself every day, ceaselessly turn away from sin, and constantly commit to live for Christ.

For Others: Perhaps many people in your life have heard about Jesus Christ or were raised in a faith tradition and have walked away. As a disciple-maker, it is your job first to pray for them, and then to be evidence of God's goodness in how you live your life. This means that your life must look different from the world. Your schedule should be centered around the things that matter to God such as prayer, relationships, and service. Your attitude should be marked by hope, not cynicism. You should be filled with integrity, which means you are the same person in private as you are in public. And people who encounter you should notice your kindness and generosity.

Pope Saint Paul VI said, "Modern man listens more willingly to witnesses than to teachers, and if he does listen to teachers, it is because they are witnesses." What we eventually say will only matter if it is backed up with how we live.

As you witness God's goodness in your life, eventually you will have to share the reason for your hope: the Gospel. In an article on discipleship, FOCUS explains, "According to Paul VI, 'There is no true evangelization if the name, the teaching, the life, the promises, the kingdom and the mystery of Jesus of Nazareth, the Son of God, are not proclaimed.' This proclamation can take several forms. However, we have found that a presentation of the Gospel itself and an explicit invitation to say 'Yes' to Jesus is one of the most effective. Acceptance of the Gospel is a crucial moment."

Suggestions:

Learn how to explain the gospel message simply so that you can use it at any time. For example, Romans 6:23 says it well: "For the wages of sin is death, but the gift of God is eternal life in Christ Jesus."

- Practice explaining the difference Jesus has made in your life in only a few sentences. It is difficult to argue with someone's experience, and people would rather hear how Christ has affected your life positively than all the reasons they "should" believe.

Keep in mind that the Lord has created you to share His message in a way that is true to your temperament and personality. Sharing the Gospel message is going to look different from person to person, yet it will share certain features. Once someone has given their life to Christ, the discipleship journey will enter into the Build phase.

Build

As a disciple continues on her journey toward spiritual maturity, knowing and believing in Jesus, she seeks to grow in intimacy with Christ and to build her life with Him at the center.

For You: A life of passionate discipleship will require you to make prayer the foundation of your life. This means that you will make time to spend silent, intimate time with God on a daily basis. Building your life around Christ also means that you seek to grow in knowledge of Him and further detachment from sin. To do this, lean into the sacraments and commit to studying the scriptures and the traditions of the Church. It is also imperative that you find someone to mentor you such as a spiritual director, or someone from your church who is farther along the journey than you are. When looking for a mentor, look for someone who is living a life of virtue, prays regularly, participates in the sacraments, and displays wisdom.

For Others: Building someone up in the faith requires quality time. A good way to help someone grow is to meet with them to pray together or study together. FOCUS describes four key habits that help to build up a disciple to live with Christ at the center of her life. They are prayer, fellowship, the sacramental life, and their formation in Christ's teachings. The more a disciple develops these habits, the more she makes herself available to think with the mind of Christ and embody His character.

Suggestions:

- Invite that person into your life so that they can see how you live. If you have kids, invite them on walks to the park, or running errands and then direct the conversation towards holy things.

- Set up a time to go to Adoration with the person you are discipling, or invite them to lead a small group with you and prep together.

- Choose a spiritual book. Read and discuss it with the person you are discipling.

- Serve together by participating in a ministry that helps the poor, volunteering at a pregnancy center, offering your time to the youth group, or serving at a local parish event.

As we build someone up in the faith by living it with them, we are modeling the Christian life for them while we build on a true friendship ordered toward Christ. Over time, we can share Christ's vision for discipleship with our friends and invite them to lead others to Christ as well. When they say yes to this, we continue the journey into the Send.

Send

Once a disciple commits to make disciples, she begins to share Christ with others. She begins to make room in her schedule to help others come to know Christ and share Him as well.

For You: When God called you to become His passionate disciple, He also called you to make disciples. A life lived on mission means that you live discipleship by introducing others to Christ, walking with them in the faith, and then teaching them how to make disciples themselves.

For Others: If someone you are discipling has committed to go on mission for Christ, help them, as a friend and mentor, to begin to disciple others.

Suggestions:

- Train them to lead a small group and then lead it with them for awhile.

- Help them figure out how and where they want to serve in the Church and then serve with them, helping them to identify opportunities to share their faith.

- Teach them how to articulate the Gospel message and share their own story of how Christ has made a difference in their lives.

- Pray with them for the people in their lives while teaching them about the journey of Win, Build, Send.

Keep in mind that while God calls everyone into His family and therefore into His mission, not everyone is ready and not everyone will say yes. Don't be phased by this problem with timing. Your job is to ask. God's work is grace. Consider the women in your community. Ask God to show you who He is calling into mission at this moment and take the steps necessary to be obedient to His call.

Appendix 6

MODERN FORMS OF SUPERSTITION, IDOLATRY AND DIVINIZATION

In Lesson 7 Day 5, we read three paragraphs from the *Catechism of the Catholic Church* on superstition (2111), idolatry (2113), and divinization (2116). Because the Lord gave us the first commandment, "You shall have no other gods before me," the *Catechism* dives deep into these issues in *CCC* 2110–2117. It is important to understand that the Catholic Church doesn't warn against certain practices and beliefs out of mere opinion. The Church's warning for us to avoid participating in anything that could lead us to worship something other than God is supported by the scriptures themselves and by thousands of years of Catholic thought and wisdom.

For a deeper understanding of practices that are incompatible with the Catholic Church's belief that there is only one God, the Christian God, and it is only He who we should worship, take a moment to read the following excerpt from the Catechism on superstition, idolatry, and divination and magic.

III. "YOU SHALL HAVE NO OTHER GODS BEFORE ME"

2110 The first commandment forbids honoring gods other than the one Lord who has revealed himself to his people. It proscribes superstition and irreligion. Superstition in some sense represents a perverse excess of religion; irreligion is the vice contrary by defect to the virtue of religion.

Superstition

2111 Superstition is the deviation of religious feeling and of the practices this feeling imposes. It can even affect the worship we offer the true God, e.g., when one attributes an importance in some way magical to certain practices otherwise lawful or necessary. To attribute the efficacy of prayers or of sacramental signs to their mere external performance, apart from the interior dispositions that they demand, is to fall into superstition.

Idolatry

2112 The first commandment condemns polytheism. It requires man neither to believe in, nor to venerate, other divinities than the one true God. Scripture constantly recalls this rejection of "idols, [of] silver and gold, the work of men's hands. They have mouths, but do not speak; eyes, but do not see." These empty idols make their worshippers empty: "Those who make them are like them; so are all who trust in them." God, however, is the "living God" who gives life and intervenes in history.

2113 Idolatry not only refers to false pagan worship. It remains a constant temptation to faith. Idolatry consists in divinizing what is not God. Man commits idolatry whenever he honors and reveres a creature in place of God, whether this be gods or demons (for example, satanism), power, pleasure, race, ancestors, the state, money, etc. Jesus says, "You cannot serve God and mammon." Many martyrs died for not adoring "the Beast," refusing even to simulate such worship. Idolatry rejects the unique Lordship of God; it is therefore incompatible with communion with God.

2114 Human life finds its unity in the adoration of the one God. The commandment to worship the Lord alone integrates man and saves him from an endless disintegration. Idolatry is a perversion of man's innate religious sense. An idolater is someone who "transfers his indestructible notion of God to anything other than God."

Divination and Magic

2115 God can reveal the future to his prophets or to other saints. Still, a sound Christian attitude consists in putting oneself confidently into the hands of Providence for whatever concerns the future, and giving up all unhealthy curiosity about it. Improvidence, however, can constitute a lack of responsibility.

2116 All forms of divination are to be rejected: recourse to Satan or demons and conjuring up the dead or other practices falsely supposed to "unveil" the future. Consulting horoscopes, astrology, palm reading, interpretation of omens and lots, the phenomena of clairvoyance, and recourse to mediums all conceal a desire for power over time, history, and, in the last analysis, other human beings, as well as a wish to conciliate hidden powers. They contradict the honor, respect, and loving fear that we owe to God alone.

2117 All practices of magic or sorcery, by which one attempts to tame occult powers, so as to place them at one's service and have a supernatural power over others—even if this were for the sake of restoring their health—are gravely contrary to the virtue of religion. These practices are even more to be condemned when accompanied by the intention of harming someone, or when they have recourse to the intervention of demons. Wearing charms is also reprehensible. Spiritism often implies divination or magical practices; the Church for her part warns the faithful against it. Recourse to so-called traditional cures does not justify either the invocation of evil powers or the exploitation of another's credulity.

With these teachings in mind, here are seven modern practices that Catholic should avoid:

1. **Crystals and Charm Wearing:** The belief that crystals, or charms possess a certain kind of luck or healing energy encourages us to place our hope in a special object instead of the God who made the object. It is a form of superstition that is widely practiced today. At best, it does nothing to lead us toward God, but at worse, it subtly leads us away from Him.

2. **Horoscopes and Astrology:** Reading horoscopes and seeking understanding of ourselves through the alignment of the stars subtly ascribes powers to the stars that belong to God only. The book of Wisdom tells us that people were enamored with creation and so began to worship creation as gods. But how much better, the writer asks, is the God who created them. Astrology often starts out as fun but can easily lead to superstition and idolatry.

3. **Seeking Mediums:** Only God knows the future. People often seek the knowledge of a medium out of despair or need to have control. Not only does this practice diminish our truth of God as the one who knows all and will work all things for our good, but it also places us in the presence of people and spirits who are opposed to God.

4. **Ouija Boards:** Ouija boards are sold as a kids game and yet Catholic priests warn that we should have nothing to do with Ouija boards. As Catholics, we believe that the devil and his demons are real and they want an opportunity to take us away from God. Ouija boards are of the Occult in nature and open up a portal for us to contend with spirits that are not of God. This is divination.

5. **Reiki:** Reiki is widely considered a popular form of healing and stress reduction. Reiki means Rei, the all-knowing God-Consciousness and Ki is

151

life-energy, which animates all living things. Reiki practitioners use a Reiki symbol to begin the healing session. Per Catholic Answers, "To "activate" a Reiki symbol, the practitioner draws the symbol in the air, or says its name, or simply visualizes it." Reiki is described as spiritual healing but the source of that healing is not the God we worship. It is divination.[32]

6. **Manifesting:** Manifesting is the belief that if we put our thoughts and desires out into the universe that we can work with the universe to bring those things to fruition in our lives. Manifesting is a form of superstition through which we attribute to the universe God-like qualities that can bring our will and desires to life. While positive thinking and taking initiative to accomplish goals in our lives are good things, the Church asks us to speak such words of desire and planning as words of prayer to God, in a spirit of cooperation with Him, asking that His will "be done on earth as it is in heaven." Manifesting teaches us to place our hope in a created thing, the universe, and to focus on serving self instead of serving God and neighbor. It is superstition and divination.

7. **Yoga:** Yoga is an immensely popular practice and the idea that Catholics should avoid it often stirs up much argument and frustration. Per Catholic Answers, the term yoga means "to yoke" in Sanskrit. This "yoking" connotes a spiritual unity, rooted in a kind of servitude. Yoga is a religious Hindu ritual through which its practitioners place themselves in poses meant to mimic the Hindu gods. The spiritual intention of the system of yoga is to unite "the union of individual consciousness with that of the Universal Consciousness."[33] The Catholic Mass, by its nature, is a spiritual practice that calls upon the presence of God and seeks to unite us with Jesus in the Eucharist. It would be impossible to separate the Mass from its purpose. It is the same with yoga. Yoga, by its nature, is a religious practice that seeks to unite the practitioner to the universal consciousness of Hinduism. Just as Catholics would consider the bodily gestures of the Sign of the Cross or genuflecting to be embodied prayers, we must understand that the gestures and movements of yoga are

---

[32] Laura Locke, "The Dangers of Reiki," Catholic Answers (1 November, 2012): https://www.catholic.com/magazine/print-edition/the-dangers-of-reiki

[33] Alexander Frank, "Should Catholics Practice Yoga", Catholic Answers (30 September, 2022): https://www.catholic.com/magazine/online-edition/should-catholics-practice-yoga

not neutral but gestures with spiritual meaning that cannot be set aside. The nature of the practice is idolatry and participating in it can connect us spiritually to what is not of God.

The Catholic Church's teachings are ultimately geared at helping us to grow close to Christ. It offers us guard rails that keep us on the path toward Him and protect us from tricks of the enemy. As it is written in 1 Peter 5:8, "Be sober, be watchful. Your adversary the devil prowls around like a roaring lion, seeking someone to devour." There is only one God. He put a lot of effort into making that clear over the course of millennia. Sin is never benign. It is never entertaining and there is nothing that these practices can do that is better for us than what following God can do for our souls. If you have participated in these practices and seek to repent of them, the Lord is waiting to offer you His mercy. If you struggle to believe that some of these are harmful, ask God to reveal to you the Truth and give you the grace to receive what He says.

If you are looking for help or healing in the folds of the Catholic Church, here are some resources that may be helpful for you.

1. Healing of Emotional and Past Wounds: John Paul II Healing Center, https://jpiihealingcenter.org
2. Post Abortive Healing: Project Rachel, https://hopeafterabortion.com
3. Prayer-centered movement: Soul Core, https://soulcore.com

Appendix 7

LECTIO DIVINA

Prepare: Find a space where you are free from distractions. Set up your space with what you might need; for example, a Bible, a journal, a pen, maybe a drink, or a lit candle. Settle your thoughts and invite the Holy Spirit in.

Come Holy Spirit. I invite You into this space. I open my heart to you. Please speak to me in the ways that only You know I need to hear and make me receptive to Your words. I love you; help me to love You more. Amen.

> John 15:5–8 "I am the vine, you are the branches. He who abides in me, and I in him, he it is that bears much fruit, for apart from me you can do nothing. If a man does not abide in me, he is cast forth as a branch and withers; and the branches are gathered, thrown into the fire and burned. If you abide in me, and my words abide in you, ask whatever you will, and it shall be done for you. By this my Father is glorified, that you bear much fruit, and so prove to be my disciples."

1. **Lectio**: read the passage once slowly. Listen and pay attention to words or phrases that stick out to you.

2. **Oratio**: read the passage again and reflect on what the Lord is trying to say to you through those words or phrases.

3. **Mediatio**: read the passage a third time and take time to respond to the Lord. What do you want to say to Him? What do you need to process? Do you need to repent or offer thanksgiving? Take time to do that.

4. **Contemplatio**: Rest in His presence. Sit in the silence for awhile and let Him work.

Lord, thank you for this time in prayer. Let me go forward loving you more deeply.

 NOTES

Answer Key

Lesson 2, Day One

1. Paul and Timothy had a close relationship. Paul called Timothy his beloved child. Paul remembered Timothy constantly in his prayers and longed night and day to see him. Timothy's presence brings Paul joy.

2. **A.** According to Paul, Timothy's sincere faith dwelt first in his grandmother, Lois, and his mother, Eunice.

    B. It takes courage to speak about your faith, and the Holy Spirit that dwelt within them was not a spirit of timidity. The Holy Spirit gave them power to speak with authority, love to speak with compassion and tenderness, and self-control to know when not to speak.

3. **A.** In 2 Timothy 1:13, Paul begged Timothy to "follow the pattern of the sound words which you have heard from me, in the faith and love which are in Christ Jesus; guard the truth that has been entrusted to you by the Holy Spirit who dwells within us."

    B. We are not to learn more about Christ just for our benefit. While we are called to be strong in the grace that is in Christ Jesus, we are to also take what we've heard and entrust it to others who are able to teach.

4. "In the last days there will come times of stress. For men will be lovers of self, lovers of money, proud, arrogant, abusive, disobedient to their parents, ungrateful, unholy... lovers of pleasure rather than lovers of God, holding the form of religion but denying the power of it...listening to anybody and never arriving at a knowledge of the truth."

Lesson 2, Day Two

1. **A.** Paul described himself as an apostle of Christ Jesus through the authority of God.

    B. In John 10:10 Jesus said that He came so that we could have abundant life. In 1 John 5:13, Saint John wants believers to know that in Christ they have eternal life.

2. **A.** He was an esteemed member of the Jewish faith of the tribe of Benjamin, a Hebrew born of Hebrews. He was a well-respected Pharisee, blameless under the law, who zealously persecuted the church.

    B. Saint Paul said he had come to regard all these things as a loss because he had met Christ. He even calls it "rubbish" or "garbage."

3. Answers will vary.

Lesson 2, Day Three

1. **A.** Saint Paul said he was grateful to God, whom he worshiped with a clear conscience just as his ancestors did. He also said that Timothy had a sincere faith that he received from his grandmother, Lois, and his mother, Eunice.

   B. Answers will vary.

2. **A.** It says that the role of parents is so important that it is almost impossible to find an adequate substitute.

   B. The *Catechism of the Catholic Church* tells us that parents should start evangelizing their kids at a young age. Parents are called to live out the gospel in their homes. They are called to teach their children to pray and help them to discover their vocation as children of God. Parents are also called to bring their children up in the life of the local parish.

3. **A.** Answers will vary.

   B. Answers will vary.

4. Answers will vary.

Lesson 2, Day Four

1. Paul told Timothy to rekindle the gift of God within him that he received from the laying on of Paul's hands.

2. **A.** The three sacraments of the church are Baptism, Confirmation, and Holy Orders. In these sacraments we receive the grace of God's divine life, but we also receive a "seal" by which the Christian shares in Christ's priesthood and is made a member of the church with different roles, according to our gifts.

   B. Fire symbolizes the transforming energy of the Holy Spirit's actions. Fire represented in the Old Testament is a "figure" for the fire of the Holy Spirit, who transforms what He touches. Fire is used all over the Bible to symbolize the transforming power of the Holy Spirit. Fire is one of the most expressive images of the Holy Spirit's actions.

3. **A.** Answers will vary.

   B. Answers will vary.

Lesson 2, Day Five

1. For God did not give us a spirit of fear but of power, love, and self-control.

2. Answers will vary

3. Answers will vary.

Lesson 3, Day One

1. **A**. He told Timothy not to be ashamed to give testimony of the Lord, not to be ashamed of Paul himself because he was a prisoner, and to be willing to suffer for the gospel, gaining strength to do so from God.

    B. Paul didn't say, "If you suffer." He spoke of suffering as inevitable—as something that is to be expected.

2. He saved us. He called us with a holy calling not according to what we have done but by His grace. He gave us His grace through Christ Jesus before the ages began.

3. **A**. God revealed his saving grace when Jesus Christ appeared. God accomplished his saving work through Christ when he abolished death and brought life and immortality back.

    B. Answers will vary.

    C. Answers will vary.

4. **A**. Grace is the free and undeserved help that God gives us to respond to his call to become children of God, adoptive sons, and partakers of the divine nature and of eternal life. Grace enables us to participate in God's trinitarian life.

    B. His vocation was to be a herald, an apostle, and a teacher.

5. Answers will vary.

Lesson 3, Day Two

1. **A**. Paul suffered because he was sharing the gospel. He said he was not ashamed because he knew God and had chosen to put his faith in Him. He also knew that God would guard what had been entrusted to him until the day that Paul would meet God at the end of his life.

    B. Answers will vary.

2. **A**. Paul told Timothy to hold to the standard of sound teaching and to guard the treasure entrusted to Timothy with the Holy Spirit's help.

    B. Answers will vary.

3. **A**. "The apostles entrusted the 'Sacred deposit' of the faith (the depositum fidei), contained in Sacred Scripture and Tradition, to the whole of the Church. 'By adhering to [this heritage] the entire holy people, united to its pastors, remains always faithful to the teaching of the apostles, to the brotherhood, to the breaking of bread and the prayers. So, in maintaining, practicing and

professing the faith that has been handed on, there should be a remarkable harmony between the bishops and the faithful.'"

B. Answers will vary.

Lesson 3, Day Three

1. Saint Paul told Timothy that everyone has turned away from him. He specifically mentioned Phygelus and Hermogenes.
2. It says that everyone fled and deserted him.
3. **A.** Answers will vary.
   B. Answers will vary.
   C. Answers will vary.
4. **A.** Saint Paul speaks of Onesiphorus. He prays for his family's household and tells Timothy that he often brought him much refreshment, was not ashamed of him, had searched for him in Rome, and was helpful at Ephesus.
   B. Answers will vary.

Lesson 3, Day Four

1. Saint Paul told Timothy to be strong in the grace of Jesus Christ and to entrust what he has learned to faithful men who will be able to teach others also.
2. **A.** Answers will vary.
   B. Answers will vary.
3. **A.** He challenged Timothy to take his share in suffering and then compared the Christian life to the life of a soldier. He told Timothy that no soldier gets entangled with civilian pursuits but stays committed to pleasing the one who enlisted him.
   B. Paul told Timothy that an athlete won't win a crown unless he competes by the rules.
   C. Answers will vary.
   D. He said that it is the hardworking farmer who ought to receive the shares of the first crops. Paul wanted us to understand that the hardworking farmer deserves the first share of the crops because it is he who has developed the discipline proper to the reward. He has gotten up early and given his entire life to his crop. He has suffered and endured hardship for the reward of a good harvest. It is the same for the Christian—the more she invests herself into the life of the gospel, the greater her reward will be.

Lesson 3, Day Five

1. Paul describes Jesus as a man who was raised from the dead and a descendant of David.
2. Answers will vary.
3. **A.** Paul reminded Timothy that he was suffering for this gospel to the point of being chained like a criminal. He then powerfully stated that the Word of God is not chained. Because of this power of God, Paul endured everything for the sake of the elect so that they might also obtain salvation in Christ Jesus.
   B. Answers will vary.

Lesson 4, Day One

1. Paul said that if we are willing to die with Jesus, we will also live with Jesus. If we endure these present sufferings, we will experience glory with Him. If we deny Him, He will deny us, but even when we are faithless, He remains faithful because he cannot deny himself.
2. Answers will vary.
3. Answers will vary.
4. Answers will vary.

Lesson 4, Day Two

1. **A.** He told Timothy to remind the people he pastored of the truths contained in that short hymn.
   B. Answers will vary.
2. **A.** He told Timothy to warn his people to avoid disputes over words. It does no good but only causes problems for those who are listening.
   B. Answers will vary.
   C. Answers will vary.
3. **A.** He told him to do his best to present himself to God as one approved by Him, a worker who has no need to be ashamed, rightly explaining the word of truth.
   B. Answers will vary.

Lesson 4, Day Three

1. **A.** He said that such people only become more and more godless and that their teachings would spread like gangrene.

B. Paul said that Hymenaeus and Philetus had deviated from the truth by saying that the resurrection had already taken place. In this instance, they were not referring to Christ's resurrection but the teaching that Christians will experience resurrection after death.

C. As Catholics, we will be raised from the dead just as Christ was raised from the dead, not only our souls but also our mortal bodies, at His second coming. This has been an essential element of the Christian faith since the beginning that we will experience.

Hymenaeus and Philetus were spreading the heresy that the resurrection of the body had either already taken place spiritually in baptism or that "resurrection" only meant that people lived on through their children. Both of these teachings went directly against the church's official teaching and caused much confusion among the faithful.[34]

2. **A.** In John 16:33, Jesus promised that in the world we will have trouble but that we should have hope because he has overcome the world.

B. Psalm 96:4–5 tells us that all religions do not lead to the same God. It tells us that the Lord made the heavens and is to be feared above all gods because other gods are idols. In John 14:6, Jesus famously says, "I am the way the truth and the life, no one comes to the Father except through me."

C. James 1:14–15 says that each person is tempted by their own desires and that desire gives birth to sin and eventually leads to death. Our sins are never harmless. They always harm someone, and they often stem from our disordered desires. Jeremiah 17:9 tells us that the heart is deceitful and corrupt. If we "follow" our hearts, we will begin to go down the wrong path.

D. If we say that we have no sin, we deceive ourselves, and the truth is not in us.

E. Paul says in Galatians 3:27–29, "as many of you who were baptized into Christ have clothed yourselves with Christ, there is no longer Jew or Greek, there is no longer slave or free, there is no longer male and female; for all of you are one in Christ Jesus." Here Paul states that our dignity is not derived from class or privilege but from the fact that we were all sinners and have been reborn into Christ. Therefore, when living in the world, we are to follow the example of Christ, who according to Philippians 2:5–8, was equal with God the Father in everything, but laid all that status and power down, emptied himself, took the

---

[34] Barclay, p.196

form of a human, and became obedient until the point of death, even death on a cross. The Christian is called to lay herself down in humble service to God and neighbor.

3. **A.** Answers will vary.

   B. Answers will vary.

Lesson 4, Day Four

1. **A.** He said that although those heresies exist, God's foundation stands firm. He knows who are His own and all who call upon His name can avoid evil.

   B. He describes the Church as a pillar and bulwark of truth.

2. **A.** Paul said that in a large house, there are utensils of silver, gold, wood, and clay. He said that some utensils are for special use and some are for ordinary use.

   B. Answers will vary.

3. All those who cleanse themselves of sin.

Lesson 4, Day Five

1. He told him to shun youthful passions and pursue righteousness, faith, love, and peace, and to do it with people who call on the Lord with a pure heart.

2. **A.** He told Timothy to have nothing to do with stupid arguments and controversies but to be kind to everyone.

   B. Answers will vary.

3. **A.** The Lord's servant must not be quarrelsome but kind to everyone—be a teacher, have patience, and correct others with gentleness.

   B. Answers will vary.

4. Paul expresses hope that God would draw people to repentance and come to know the truth through Christian kindness. He hoped that God would grant that they'd repent and escape the devil's snare, no longer being captive to his will.

Lesson 6, Day One

1. **A.** Paul wanted Timothy to understand that in the last days, distressing times will come.

   B. No one, not even Jesus while He was on earth, knew the time of His second coming and the end of the world as we know it.

2. **A.** The Church tells us that we have been in the final age of the world since Christ's Ascension into Heaven. It says the "final age of the world is with

us, and the renewal of the world is irrevocably under way...the Church is endowed already with a certain sanctity that is real but imperfect." This age began after Christ's Ascension.

B. Jesus said that it is precisely because we do not know when He will return that we should keep awake and be ready. Jesus compared this alertness to the owner of a house who would have protected his house if he had known when a robber would break in. He calls us to understand the time that we live in and to stay awake to how evil and good are both moving in the world so that we will be ready for His return, whether it is our last day or the end of the age.

C. Answers will vary.

3. Paul said that people will be lovers of themselves, lovers of money, proud, arrogant, abusive, disobedient to their parents, ungrateful, unholy, inhuman, implacable, slanderers, profligates, brutes, and haters of the good.

Lesson 6, Day Two

1. **A.** Answers will vary.
   B. Answers will vary.
   C. Answers will vary.
2. **A.** In the last days, God will pour out His Spirit upon all flesh.
   B. Paul said that where sin increases, grace increases all the more. Sin exercised dominion over death, but grace exercises dominion through justification that leads us to eternal life in Christ Jesus.
3. Answers will vary.

Lesson 6, Day Three

1. Paul said that people will be treacherous, reckless, swollen with conceit, and lovers of pleasure instead of lovers of God.
2. Paul said that many live as enemies of the cross of Christ. He said their end is their destruction, their god is their bellies, their glory is their shame, and their minds are set on earthly things.
3. **A.** Answers will vary.
   B. Answers will vary.
4. **A.** 1 Corinthians 10:31 says that no matter what we are doing, we should glorify God while doing it. This means that when we enjoy God's created things, we

should do so in a way that leads us to worship Him because He is so good to share it with us.

    B. Answers will vary.

5. **A.** They will hold the outward form of godliness but deny its power.

    B. Answers will vary.

Lesson 6, Day Four

1. Paul said they were going into the household and captivating silly women who were overwhelmed by their sins and swayed by all kinds of desires.

2. **A.** He describes them as being tossed to and fro and blown about by every wind of doctrine by people's trickery and their deceitful scheming.

    B. Answers will vary.

3. **A.** He described these women as always desiring instruction but never arriving at the knowledge of the truth.

    B. Answers will vary.

Lesson 6, Day Five

1. **A.** Paul compares these people, the ones who exhibit deceitful behavior and draw others into deceptive beliefs, to Jannes and Jambres who were, according to Jewish tradition, the magicians who opposed Moses in Pharaoh's court. Paul knew that these people will not make progress because their folly will become plain to everyone.

    B. "He who is in you is greater than he who is in the world" (1 John 4:4).

2. They were described as men of corrupt mind and counterfeit faith.

3. **A.** The opposite of a corrupt mind is a mind renewed and enlightened by God's truth. In Romans 12:2, Paul challenges his reader to "not conform to the pattern of this world, but be transformed by the renewing of your mind." In Ephesians 1:18, Paul prays that "the eyes of your heart may be enlightened, so that you will know what is the hope of His calling, what are the riches of the glory of His inheritance in the saints." An enlightened mind has hope. That hope is based on all that Christ has done for us.

    B. Answers will vary. One of the main ways that the Church suggests we cultivate and renew our intellect is through mental prayer, spending time in silence praying through scripture or simply being with God daily. The purpose of mental prayer is to allow the Lord to weed out our vices and replace them with His virtues, i.e., to be rid of worldly, ungodly values and thinking and conform our minds and behaviors to His. The more faithful we are to spending time with God in mental prayer, the more space we give God to facilitate this renewal.

4. **A.** Genuine, authentic, real, sincere, true.

   B. In 1 Peter 1:6–7, we are encouraged to rejoice in suffering. It says, "In this you rejoice, though now for a little while you may have to suffer various trials, so that the genuineness of your faith, more precious than gold which though perishable is tested by fire, may redound to praise and glory and honor at the revelation of Jesus Christ."

   C. Answers will vary.

Lesson 7, Day One

1. **A.** Timothy observed Paul's teaching, conduct, aim in life, faith, patience, love, and steadfastness.

   B. Imitate me as I imitate Christ.

   C. Answers will vary.

   D. Answers will vary.

2. Timothy also followed Paul through his persecutions and sufferings, especially in Antioch, Iconium, and Lystra. Paul said that the Lord rescued him from it all.

3. Answers will vary.

Lesson 7, Day Two

1. **A.** He believed that all who want to live a godly life will be persecuted.

   B. Answers will vary.

2. **A.** Those who refuse to follow God will go from bad to worse, deceiving others and being deceived.

   B. Answers will vary.

3. Answers will vary.

Lesson 7, Day Three

1. **A.** Paul called Timothy to a different standard of living by saying, "But as for you." He then told him to continue in what he had learned and firmly believed and to remember where he had learned it in his childhood and how he would

have been acquainted with the sacred writings (the Old Testament), which instruct in salvation through faith in Jesus Christ.

   B. Moses told the Israelites to keep the words that he was commanding them. He told them to recite them to their children at home, when they were away, when they lay down, and when they rose. He also told them to bind God's commands to their hands, foreheads, doorposts, and gates.

2. **A.** Answers will vary.
   B. Answers will vary.

3. **A.** Paul said, "All scripture is inspired by God and profitable for teaching, reproof, correction, training in righteousness, that man of God may be complete and equipped for every good work."

   B. According to *CCC* 101, God in his goodness condescended to speak to humanity in human words the truth about himself. In *CCC* 105 and 106, the Church teaches that God is the author of sacred scripture, which was written down by the inspiration of the Holy Spirit. He inspired human authors to compose sacred scripture. He acted through them and by them, writing what He wanted and no more.

4. Answers will vary.

Lesson 7, Day Four

1. In 2 Timothy 1, Paul gave Timothy a solemn charge, or urge, according to other translations of the Bible. He did this in the presence of God and Jesus, whom he described as the judge of the living and the dead.

2. He wanted Timothy to be aware that Christ will one day return, ushering in His kingdom.

3. **A.** He told Timothy to proclaim the message; to be persistent whether the time is favorable or unfavorable; and to convince, rebuke, and encourage with the utmost patience in teaching.
   B. Answers will vary.
   C. Answers will vary.

4. **A.** Answers will vary.
   B. Answers will vary.
   C. Answers will vary.

Lesson 7, Day Five

1. Paul explains that there is a time coming in which people will not tolerate the Truth but will have itching ears, always looking for and finding a teacher that will satisfy their own desires.

2. Because of original sin, we are deprived of original holiness and justice. Human nature hasn't been completely corrupted, but it has been wounded. Humans suffer ignorance, pain, unhappiness, sorrow, and they are inclined to sin, which is called concupiscence. Baptism turns us back toward God, but our inclination toward evil persists. Because of the wound of sin, it is harder for us to follow God than it is for us to follow our own way into sin.

   God gives us our Catholic faith as a vast treasury, but when we get a glimpse of what the world offers, it seems much better, much more fun, and much more fulfilling. Before we truly know and love God, He seems to be against us, standing over our shoulder and telling us no. And even after we begin to follow Him, His goodness can appear to us as mostly humble, unflashy, and unpowerful. He calls us to the narrow road, the harder way that will eventually lead us to true life. Our perception is that He is holding out on us, unable to be trusted, so we gravitate toward temptation. Every other message seems to be better and more for us, so it corresponds to our tendency to ignore Jesus' call and follow the wide road, the path set by the world that eventually leads to destruction.

3. **A.** They will wander away into myths.

   B. Superstition. Superstition happens when someone attributes importance or magic to practices that would otherwise be lawful or necessary.

   Idolatry. Idolatry happens when we divinize what is not God. We commit idolatry when we honor creatures or things in place of God.

   Divinization. Divination is taking recourse to Satan or demons. It also includes consulting horoscopes, astrologers, palm readers, and mediums. They contradict the love we are supposed to have for God alone.

   C. Answers will vary.

4. He tells Timothy to be sober, endure suffering, do the work of the evangelist, and carry out the ministry fully.

Lesson 8, Day One

1. **A.** Paul says that he is being poured out like a libation and that the time of his departure has come.

   B. Paul compared the Christian life to a race in which runners compete. He said many compete, but only one receives the price. He also said that athletes train hard to receive a perishable crown, but Christians are racing for an imperishable one. Therefore, we should run our races with a commitment to win.

2. Paul says that he has fought the good fight, he has finished the race, and he has kept the faith.

3. **A.** According to Hebrews 10: 36–37, we are called to endure in doing God's will. God says he takes no pleasure in the one who shrinks back from Him. We are called not to shrink back but to stay close to God, continue to trust, and have faith.

   B. By contrast, the fruit of the Spirit is love, joy, peace, patience, kindness, generosity, faithfulness, gentleness, and self-control. There is no law against such things.

   C. We are called to be Christ's witness, to the ends of the earth.

4. **A.** Answers will vary.

   B. Answers will vary.

Lesson 8, Day Two

1. Paul said that there is a crown of righteousness awaiting him. The Lord holds it for him and all who long for His appearing.

2. Jesus promised that if we remain faithful until death, we will receive a crown of life.

3. The *Catechism of the Catholic Church* describes Heaven as perfect life with the Trinity, the Virgin Mary, and all the saints. In Heaven, our deepest human longings will be supremely fulfilled. *CCC* 1025 tells us that to live in Heaven is to live with Christ. We will live "in Christ" but retain our true identity and name.

4. Answers will vary.

Lesson 8, Day Three

1. **A.** He told Timothy to do his best to come to him quickly.

   B. Paul said that Demas had fallen in love with the world and abandoned him, and that Crescens was in Galatia and Titus in Dalmatia.

   C. Answers will vary.

2. **A.** Luke was with him, and Paul asked for Timothy to bring Mark because he would be useful to Paul.

    B. Paul and Barnabas were going to return to the cities where they had already proclaimed the Gospel to see how they are doing. Barnabas wanted to take John Mark on the journey, but Paul refused. He no longer trusted him since John Mark had abandoned them on an earlier journey. Paul and Barnabas had a major disagreement that resulted in their separation.

    C. Answers will vary.

3. Paul asked Timothy to bring him his cloak and scrolls that he had left with another church member named Carpus.

4. Alexander betrayed him, but Paul said that it would be God who repaid him, not Paul. He then warned Timothy not to trust him. Romans 12:19 gives insight into Paul's integrity. In this verse, Paul writes, "Beloved, never avenge yourselves, but leave it to the wrath of God; for it is written, 'Vengeance is mine, I will repay, says the Lord.'" This is the example we are to follow with people who have harmed us. We are not to seek vengeance; rather, commit those who have hurt us to God's justice, and set ourselves free through forgiveness.

Lesson 8, Day Four

1. Paul said that at his first defense, no one showed up to support him. He said, "let it not be held against them."

2. Paul said the Lord stood by him and gave him strength to proclaim the word fully, that all the gentiles would hear it. He also said that he was rescued from the lion's mouth, that the Lord will rescue him from every evil and save him for His heavenly kingdom.

3. **A.** In Psalm 22, the psalmist proclaims that the Lord is not far off. He then asks the Lord to deliver him from the sword, the dog, the mouth of the lion, and the wild oxen. In 2 Timothy 4:17–18, Paul proclaims that the Lord stood by him, gave him help, delivered him from the lion, and will also rescue him from every evil.

    B. Answers will vary.

    C. Answers will vary.

4. Paul said in Romans 8:35–38 that nothing can separate us from the love of Christ. Not tribulation, not distress, persecution, famine, nakedness, peril, or sword. He said that in all of it, Christians are more than conquerors; not death, nor life, nor spiritual powers, nor distance, nor anything else can separate us from the love of Christ.

5. Answers will vary.

Lesson 8, Day Five

1. Paul told Timothy to greet Prisca, Aquila, the household of Onesiphorus, Erastus, and Trophimus. He also sent greetings to Timothy from Eubulus, Pudens, Linus, and Claudia. He completed his letter by saying: "The Lord be with your spirit. Grace be with you."

2. Answers will vary.

3. **A.** Answers will vary.
    B. Answers will vary.
    C. Answers will vary.

4. **A.** Answers will vary.
    B. Answers will vary.
    C. Answers will vary.

Prayer Pages

walking with purpose

Passionate Discipleship Prayers

Dear Jesus,

Help me to spread your fragrance *everywhere* I go. Flood my soul with your spirit and life. Penetrate and possess my whole being so utterly that all my life may only be a radiance of yours. Shine through me, and be so in me that every soul I come in contact with may feel your presence in my soul. Let them look up and see no longer me but only Jesus. Stay with me, and then I shall begin to shine as you shine, so to shine as to be a light to others. Let me praise you in the way you love best by shining on those around me. Let me preach you without preaching, not by words but by my example. Amen.

—*Saint John Henry Newman*

May Mary, Mother of the Church, Star of Evangelization, accompany us on our journey. As you remained with the disciples on the day of Pentecost, remain with us. To you do we turn with confidence. Through your intercessions, may the Lord grant us the gift of perseverance in our missionary duty, which is a matter for the entire Church community. Amen.

—adapted from *Pope Saint John Paul II's Message for World Mission Sunday, 2001*

Prayer Requests

Date:

* * *

Date:

Prayer Requests

Date:

Date:

Prayer Requests

Date:

Date:

Prayer Requests

Date:

Date:

Prayer Requests

Date:

Journal Your Prayers & Grow Closer to God

The Walking with Purpose *Praying from the Heart: Guided Prayer Journal* is a beautiful, comprehensive prayer journal that provides a private space to share your thoughts and feelings with the Lord.

Journaling your prayers lets you express a greater depth of intimacy toward God, and it will help you cultivate the practice of gratitude. Journaling will motivate you to pray regularly, too!

Praying from the Heart lays flat for easy writing, and is fashioned after the way that author Lisa Brenninkmeyer journals her own prayers. You'll love the deluxe linen hard cover with embossed gold lettering, and many other special details.

shop.walkingwithpurpose.com

walking with purpose

SO MUCH MORE THAN A BIBLE STUDY

Walking with Purpose Devotionals

Daily affirmations of God's love

Rest: 31 Days of Peace

- A beautiful, hardcover, pocket-sized devotional to take wherever you go.

- 31 Scripture-based meditations that you can read (and re-read) daily.

- Become saturated with the truth that you are seen, known, and loved by a God who gave everything for you!

Be Still: A Daily Devotional to Quiet Your Heart

- Grow closer to the Lord each day of the year with our 365-day devotional.

- This beautifully designed hardcover devotional collection will renew your mind and help you look at things from God's perspective.

- Apply what you read in *Be Still*, and you'll make significant progress in your spiritual life!

shop.walkingwithpurpose.com

walking with purpose

SO MUCH MORE THAN A BIBLE STUDY

The guided tour of God's love begins here.

Opening Your Heart: The Starting Point begins a woman's exploration of her Catholic faith and enhances her relationship with Jesus Christ. This Bible study is designed to inspire thoughtful consideration of the fundamental questions of living a life in the Lord. More than anything, it's a weekly practice of opening your heart to the only One who can heal and transform lives.

Explore these topics and more:

- What is the role of the Holy Spirit in my life?
- What does the Eucharist have to do with my friendship with Christ?
- What are the limits of Christ's forgiveness?
- Why and how should I pray?
- What is the purpose of suffering?
- What challenges will I face in my efforts to follow Jesus more closely?
- How can fear be overcome?

A companion video series complements this journey with practical insights and spiritual support.

Opening Your Heart is a foundational 22-lesson Bible study that serves any woman who seeks to grow closer to God. It's an ideal starting point for women who are new to Walking with Purpose and those with prior practice in Bible study, too.

To share Walking with Purpose with the women in your parish, contact us at walkingwithpurpose.com/contact-us.

walkingwithpurpose.com

Our Mission

Enabling women to know Christ
personally through Scripture.

Our Vision

Our vision for the future is that as more Catholic
women and girls deepen their relationships with
Jesus Christ, eternity-changing transformation will take
place in their hearts—and, by extension—in their families,
in their communities, and ultimately, in our world.

walking with purpose

You can support our mission through a tax-deductible gift.
Learn more at walkingwithpurpose.com/donate